Christianity and Evolution

By Pierre Teilhard de Chardin

Pierre Teilhard de Chardin

Christianity
and Evolution

Translated by René Hague

A Harvest Book • Harcourt, Inc.

A Helen and Kurt Wolff Book

San Diego   New York   London

The essay " How I Believe"
was first published in English translation
in 1969 by Collins, London,
and Harper & Row, New York.

Library of Congress Cataloguing-in-Publication Data
Teilhard de Chardin, Pierre
Christianity and evolution
(A Harvest book.)
"A Helen and Kurt Wolff book.'
Translation of Comment je crois
Includes bibiographical references.
1. Theology — Addresses, essays, lectures
I. Title
[BR85.T3313 1974] 201'.I 73-12926
ISBN 0-15-602818-2

Printed in the United States of America
First Harvest edition 1974

B D F H J I G E C A

CONTENTS

FOREWORD

It was originally intended that this tenth volume [in the French edition] of the works of Père Teilhard de Chardin should contain all his essays and articles dealing with theological problems. However, the number and length of these writings are such that it has been necessary, to avoid producing an unreasonably large volume, to divide them into two volumes, the first of which will contain writings that are more particularly concerned with speculative theology, while the second will bring together those in which Christian life is the dominant subject. There must, it is true, be some arbitrariness in such a division, particularly when one remembers that in the same essay or article Père Teilhard often deals with both aspects of the theological problem. Whatever reservations one may have about the decision, we feel nevertheless that the selection presented in this volume has the advantage of bringing out with equal clarity both the theoretical and the practical aspect of the author's theological thought.

In recent years much has been published about Teilhard de Chardin's theological writings, both about his theology as a whole and about particular points in his teaching. We may mention, for example, the studies of Père Henri de Lubac,[1] of Georges Crespy,[2] Piet Smulders,[3] Christopher

1. *The Religion of Teilhard de Chardin* (Collins, London, and Desclée, New York, 1967); *The Faith of Teilhard de Chardin* (Burns & Oates, London, 1965).

2. *La Pensée théologique de Teilhard de Chardin* (Ed. Universitaires, Paris, 1961); *De la science à la théologie, Essai sur Teilhard de Chardin* (Neuchâtel, 1965).

3. *Het visioen van Teilhard de Chardin* (Brugge, 1964; French trans., Desclée de Brouwer, Paris, 1967).

Mooney,[4] Sigurd Daecke,[5] Eulalio Baltazar,[6] Robert North,[7] Denis Mermod,[8] Robert Francœur,[9] George Maloney,[10] E. Martinazzo,[11] Robert Faricy,[12] and Francisco Bravo.[13] To this confessedly incomplete list should be added a large number of shorter studies, articles and reports of congresses, at which Teilhard's theological thought was the subject of many papers and much discussion. Particularly noteworthy among these was the International Scotist Congress, held at Oxford and Edinburgh from 11 to 17 September 1966, when several papers were concerned with Père Teilhard's Christology.[14] Seldom in the history of theology has a writer's thought been the occasion, in so few years, of so much often passionate study and discussion. This is all the more remarkable in that Père Teilhard never put himself forward as a theologian and regarded his theological essays rather as mere suggestions. The number and the quality of the studies devoted to his work in this field – inspired at times by very different aims and principles – make

4. *Teilhard de Chardin and the Mystery of Christ* (Collins, London, and Harper & Row, New York, 1966).

5. *Teilhard de Chardin und die Evangelische Theologie* (Vandenhoeck & Ruprecht, Göttingen, 1967).

6. *Teilhard and the Supernatural* (Helicon, Baltimore, 1966).

7. *Teilhard and the Creation of the Soul* (Bruce, Milwaukee, 1967).

8. *La Morale de Teilhard* (Paris, 1967).

9. *Perspectives in Evolution* (Helicon, Baltimore, 1965).

10. *The Cosmic Christ. From Paul to Teilhard* (Sheed & Ward, New York, 1968).

11. *Teilhard de Chardin. Conamen lecturae criticae* (Rome, 1965).

12. *Teilhard de Chardin's Theology of the Christian in the World* (Sheed & Ward, New York, 1967).

13. *Christ in the Thought of Teilhard de Chardin* (University of Notre Dame Press, Nelson, 1967).

14. *De doctrina Joannis Duns Scoti. Acta Congressus Scotistici Internationalis Oxonii et Edimburgi 11-17 Sept. 1966 celebrati*, Vol. III: *Problemata Theologica* (Studia Scholastico-Scotistica, Vol. III), Rome, 1968. (See in particular the papers by Robert North, Gabriele Allegra and Gerardo Cardaropoli.)

it abundantly clear how insistently Père Teilhard's thought has captured the attention of theologians and what an unusually powerful stimulus it is to the theological speculation of our day.

It is not possible in this short foreword to analyse the works just referred to, nor to offer any judgment on the problems under discussion. It may be as well, however, to say a word to those who are not professional theologians, which may help them better to understand what Teilhard was really trying to do and what is the real significance of what he had to say in this connexion.

In order fully to understand a writer, we must do more than examine the various points in the teaching he offers. The first thing we have to do is to form as clear a picture as we can of the problem to which the teaching is presumed to supply a solution. If we ask what is the central problem with which Teilhard was concerned, the problem which is the core of his theological thought, it would be generally agreed that it was without doubt what is now known as secularization. The phrase 'religion of the earth' ('the God of the Ahead') which Teilhard uses, and the secularization so much discussed by modern theologians cover, in fact, the same ideological and sociological reality. To keep things quite clear, we should be careful to distinguish between secularity, secularization, and secularism. By *secularity* is commonly meant recognition of the value inherent in the earth and in man's earthly activity – that human activity of which the most important part is, in this age, constituted by science, technology and the organization of society. By *secularization* we mean the historical and socio-logical process which led to this recognition, and which is characterized by a progressive enfranchisement, in man's scientific and political activity, from any interference on the part of theology and metaphysics. By *secularism*, finally, we mean every attitude or teaching which stresses exclusively the values of earthly life at the expense of any religious or metaphysical consideration.

All secularism, it goes without saying, is unacceptable to the Christian, but what should be the Christian's attitude to the undeniable fact of secularization? How are we to define the relationship between the message of the gospel and the 'religion of the earth'? How are we to effect in our own selves the reconciliation of our earthly task and our heavenly vocation? This is, of course, no new problem in theology, but it has never made itself felt so acutely as in our own day. Teilhard took it as the starting-point of his theological reflection, at a time when few of us realized the urgency of the problem. With the backing of his experience as a scientist and his exceptional sensitivity to the spiritual currents of our age, he realized how fully modern man had awoken to a clear awareness of his earthly vocation and responsibilities. With astonishing insight, he foresaw that this current must inevitably lead not only to a widening of the gap between the Church and modern culture, but also to a crisis in the very heart of the believing world. What is going on, he tells us, is 'the irresistible rise in the human sky, through all the avenues of thought and action, of an evolutive God of the Ahead – hostile, at first glance, to the transcendent God of the Above whom Christianity offers for our worship.' 'So long', he continues, 'as the Church neglects, by means of a refashioned Christology (all the elements of which are available to us), to solve the apparent conflict that henceforth exists between the traditional God of revelation and the "new" God of evolution, so long, too, will there be an increasing distress not only on the fringe of the believing world but at its very core; and, *pari passu*, Christianity's power to attract and convert will grow less.'[15]

What Teilhard foresaw in that passage, and in many others, is now without any doubt becoming a reality; and we may

15. Below, p. 212.

well wonder whether we would not be closer today to finding a solution if his warnings had been heeded at the right time. However that may be, there is no doubt about the fundamental accuracy of his diagnosis: the crisis we are suffering today does indeed consist in the conflict between a religion of transcendence and a secularized world, between the 'God of the Above' and the 'God of the Ahead', between a 'religion of heaven' and a 'religion of the earth'.

Yet, while the problem of secularity, as we meet it now, is already central to Teilhard's thought, he gives it an extremely original form and dimension. This is because in Teilhard man's earthly work is linked to the idea of a world in evolution. In a static world the dignity of human labour does not qualify for expression in the same terms as it does in a world in evolution. It is precisely because we live in a world which is in process of construction that our labour takes on a new value and a capital importance. Man's task coincides exactly with the duty to carry out the great work of evolution and guide it to completion. Teilhard, therefore, was perfectly justified in exalting the greatness and the dignity of that work and in speaking of a 'holy love of earth' long before Dietrich Bonhoeffer spoke of a 'holy secularity' or worldliness (*heilige Weltlichkeit*).

Further, just as in Teilhard we meet the problem of secularity in a new and extremely rich form, so the solution he offers differs radically from that put forward by the majority of secularity theologians such as, among others, Harvey Cox, William Hamilton, Thomas Altizer, or Paul Van Buren. Far from leaning towards a Godless theology or surrendering, as is fashionable in some quarters, to a radical secularism, Teilhard felt that the solution of this problem was to be found at the very centre of the Christian faith, in an updated Christology. The universe whose greatness and richness we admire has no existence outside Christ; it is organically linked to Christ in the sense that everything has been created for Christ and finds its fulfilment in him.

This Christology, of strongly Pauline inspiration, has much in common with what is often called Scotism, even though it diverges from Scotism on a number of important points. Duns Scotus takes God as his starting-point and asks what was the divine intention in decreeing the incarnation of the Word. Teilhard considers the value of the world and asks how it can be related to the incarnate Word. In the speculation of the medieval theologian the emphasis is more on the pre-existence of Christ in relation to all future creation. Teilhard was to emphasize eschatology, the term for earthly history of which Christ will be the final and permanent consecration. For Duns Scotus, Christ is primarily the first conceived in the divine thought of creation; for Teilhard he is primarily the term and supreme culmination of history.

Such a Christology, in Teilhard's view, contains the true solution to the problem of secularity. If man's vocation consists in building the earth and if that building is the preparation – insufficient, indeed, but essential – for the coming of Christ, it must necessarily follow that human labour, in its richest and highest manifestation, is intrinsically orientated towards Christ, the end and crown of this world-in-formation. This connexion between human labour and the Christ of the parousia was the central theme of Teilhard's earlier publication, *Le Milieu Divin* (*The Divine Milieu*). The essays and articles that follow provide fuller elucidation of certain points in Teilhard's teaching on which *Le Milieu Divin* was based. It will be apparent that he put the theological problem of secularity in an extremely original and illuminating form and at the same time provided a truly Christian solution that fits in completely with the faith handed down by tradition.

Teilhard is no advocate of the current of secularism from which our difficulties arise; he urges us to go beyond every form of secularism by including the values of the earth in a Christocentric vision of the world.

Apart from Christological questions, most of the essays in this volume deal primarily with the problem of original sin. Any informed reader will realize that what he will find are essays which Teilhard intended and hoped would be examined more closely by professional theologians. While some of his suggestions may still seem somewhat tentatively expressed, there can nevertheless be little doubt that it is in the direction he indicates that theological research on this subject is being pursued.

N. M. Wildiers,
Docteur en Théologie.

NOTE ON THE PHYSICAL
UNION BETWEEN THE HUMANITY
OF CHRIST AND THE FAITHFUL
IN THE COURSE OF THEIR
SANCTIFICATION

WE may distinguish *a priori* (and meet *a posteriori* in different theological and mystical currents) three different tendencies in the ways of explaining how Christ *'vitis et vita vera'*,[1] Christ *'caput creationis et ecclesiae'*,[2] acts upon the faithful in the course of their sanctification. There are some Christians who understand Christ's saving influence primarily by analogy with our moral, juridical, categorical forms of causality; with, that is, some suggestion of the letter of the law, of something imposed from outside. Others, however, are more inclined to look at the 'natural', intrinsic, side of things, and try to explain Christ's action as experienced by us by relating it chiefly to the physical and organic causalities of the universe. These latter fall, again, into two classes: those who attach the vivifying action upon souls above all to the Word, in Jesus Christ – and those who tend to attribute as large as possible a part in this physical operation to the humanity of our Lord.

It calls for no great experience of the Christian soul to see that the last of these three tendencies – that which tends to magnify (to 'emphasize')[3] the physical links between Christ's humanity and ourselves – is particularly vigorous today.

The object of this note is to indicate a possible way of under-

1. 'The vine and the true life', after John 15:1 and 14:6.
2. 'The head of creation and of the Church', after Col. 1:18: 'He is the head of the body, the Church'.
3. Teilhard uses the English word.

standing and establishing this thesis – accepted in practice by many Christians in their interior life – that the holiness of the Christian develops and is completed in a sort of contact (physical and permanent) with the *actually human* reality of Christ the Saviour.

A solid basis for the demonstration, or rather the suggestions, we have in mind may profitably be sought in a consideration of the consummated mystical body (that is, the Pauline pleroma). In the first place, since the pleroma is the kingdom of God in its completed form, the properties attributed to it by Scripture must be regarded as specially characteristic of the entire supernatural organism, even if they are to be found only in an ill-defined form in any particular preparatory phase of beatification. Secondly, in no other reality is the physical and personal action of the theandric Christ made manifest to us by revelation more than in the Church triumphant. When we try to sum up the Church's teaching and the thought of the saints on the innermost nature of beatitude, we find that in heaven both Christ and the elect must be regarded as forming one living whole, disposed in a strict hierarchic pattern. Each elect soul, it is true, possesses God directly, and finds in that unique possession the fulfilment of his own individuality. But, however *individual* this possession of the divine, this contact, may be, they are not obtained *individually*. The beatific vision, which illuminates each of the elect for himself alone, is at the same time *a collective act* performed by the whole mystical organism at once 'per modum unius potentiae' (as one single force). The organ made for seeing God is not (if you get to the bottom of the dogma) the isolated human soul; it is the human soul united to all the other souls, under the humanity of Christ. We attain God in heaven 'sicuti est' (as he is), but in the measure in which we are assumed by Christ into the mystical extensions of his substance. Briefly, the state of beatitude must be understood as a state of *permanent eucharistic union* in which we will be raised up and maintained *as a body* (that is to say *'per modum unius'* – as one single being) and *'in corpore Christi'* (in the body of Christ). This explains the fundamental relationship between the eucharist and charity, between love of God and love of our neighbour.

If this is indeed the condition of holiness *'in termino'* (at its term), that is to say a union with God in Jesus-Christ-Man, it would appear that there is only one way in which we can understand the nature of holiness *'in via'* (on its road to that term): in which, that is, we can understand our sanctification as it is here and now laboriously being effected. Since beatification coincides with a certain degree of physical incorporation in the created being of our Lord, we must inevitably admit that in the course of his meritorious life the believer is introduced into, and progresses further in, a certain state of physical connexion with the humanity of Christ the Saviour. If we are not to establish an unwarranted disparity between the state of grace and the state of glory, we must say that grace does more than attach us by its spiritual instillation to the divinity of the Word: it brings with it a certain progressive inclusion in a created organism, physically centred on the humanity of Christ.

Far from conflicting with the eucharist or serving as a repetition of the eucharist, this 'habitual' communion effected by sanctifying grace between Christ and the faithful gives its full significance, we should note, to sacramental reception of the sacred species.

In the first place, it is quite certain that the eucharist, of which many of the elect will have been unable to partake during their life on earth, is not the only means by which the faithful can achieve contact – contact which is necessary as a 'necessary' means – with Christ's humanity: the contact which is to ensure their integration in the pleroma. We become members of Christ before any external contact with his sacramental body.

Moreover, it is equally clear that in receiving the eucharist, adherence to the flesh of Christ, as produced by consuming the species, is effected *on a physical plane that is very different* from that on which the evident quantitative contact between our body and the Host takes place. Is it not, in fact, precisely at the moment when this quantitative contact would tend to be fully established (by assimilation) that the species undergo corruption and the divine presence becomes less marked?

The eucharist, in short, can be fully explained only in terms of a mode of contact with Christ which is much more independent of time and lower matter than that of the crudely material confluence between the sacred species and ourselves.

In that case, how should we approximately represent eucharistic (sacramental) union? – simply as the tightening, specially chosen and favoured, and wonderfully active, of a looser (but real) link established and maintained '*perenniter*' (constantly) by the state of grace. Long before any communion, a first and *permanent* connexion through the operation of baptism is formed between the Christian and the body of Christ. And after each communion, in spite of the disappearance of the sacred species which had, for a time, raised it to a special degree of intimacy and importance, this connexion persists – more strongly established, even though in a less concentrated form.

If we understand the matter in this way, sacramental communion ceases to be a discontinuous element in Christian life and becomes the fabric from which it is woven. It is the accentuation and the renewal of a permanent state which attaches us continuously to Christ. In short, the Christian's whole life, on earth as in heaven, can be seen as a sort of perpetual eucharistic union. The Divine comes to us only as 'informed' by Christ Jesus: that is the fundamental law of our supernatural life.

The immediate practical corollary of this law is that, *for the just man*, God's general presence is constantly backed by a particular presence of Christ '*secundum suam naturam humanam*' (according to his human nature) – a presence which is prior (*in ordine naturae*, in the order of nature) to the indwelling of the divine persons in the sanctified soul. But this is not all: since this presence grows in proportion with the state of grace in us, it is capable not only of enduring but also of being *intensified* by the whole miscellaneous body of what we do and what we suffer. It is literally true that '*quidquid agit Christianus, Christus agitur*' – whatever the Christian does, it is to Christ it is done. Considerations of this order are obviously of great importance in mysticism: they justify us in believing that we can, in strict fact, live always and everywhere without being separated from Jesus Christ.

The more familiar we become with this idea of a physical influx continually emanating (with an admixture of grace) for souls from the humanity of Christ, the more we realize how closely it harmonizes with the very numerous scriptural passages in which our possession of the Father is strictly subordinated to our *permanent* union with the incarnate Word; the more wonderful, too, become the depth and clarity of the evangelical precepts, in particular those which insist on communion and charity. To love one's brothers and to receive the body of Christ is not simply to obey and merit a reward: it is organically to build up, element by element, the living unity of the pleroma in Christ.

No serious disadvantage can be set against the numerous advantages that accrue to the interior life from as realistic as possible a conception of the links which attach our being to that of Christ.

In the first place, when we extend all around us the domain of Christ's humanity we have no reason to fear that we are veiling from ourselves the face of the Godhead. Since we adhere to Christ '*in ordine vitali*' – in the order of life – he is *not an intermediary* separating us from God, but a *medium* uniting us to God. '*Philippe, qui videt me, videt Patrem*' – 'He who has seen me, Philip, has seen the Father.'[4]

Nor need we fear, again, that we are putting too great a strain on the limits that define the lower nature in which the Word is incarnate. However boundless the power we must attribute to this nature if its influence is to radiate continually over each one of us, such magnitude should not alarm us. By the horizons it opens up for us on to the power hidden within created being, and more particularly on to the heart of Jesus Christ, this overplus is seen to be, on the contrary, one of the most magnetic aspects of . . . (*Unfinished. The missing word appears to be 'Christianity'.*)

> Unpublished, not dated. It appears to have been written in January 1920.

4. John 14:9.

ON THE NOTION OF CREATIVE
TRANSFORMATION

SCHOLASTICISM distinguishes, to my knowledge, only two sorts of variations in being (movement).

1. Creation, that is to say 'productio entis *ex nihilo* sui et *subjecti*'.[1]

2. Transformation, that is to say 'productio entis ex nihilo sui et *potentia subjecti*'.[2]

Thus for Scholasticism creation and transformation are two absolutely heterogeneous and mutually *exclusive* modes of movement within the concrete reality of one and the same act.

This absolute separation of the two notions means that we have to regard the formation of the world as being effected in two completely distinct 'phases':

1. Initially, the placing outside nothingness (*extra nihilum*) of a certain body of potencies (the initial creative phase).

2. Next, an autonomous development of these potencies, maintained by 'conservation' (the phase of transformation by secondary causes).

3. Finally, new placings outside nothingness (*extra nihilum*) each time the historical development of the world shows us

---

1. 'Production of being out of nothing (without pre-existence of self or subjacent)'. The classic formula in Scholastic philosophy: '*Productio rei ex nihilo sui et subjecti*', means that the created substance is drawn in its entirety (matter and form) from nothingness. Nothing pre-exists: neither the thing itself in its formal perfection, nor a matter from which and in which the form could be produced (matter that would be the subject of a transformation). God produces the universe without using anything else, through his almighty will.

2. 'Production of being without pre-existence of self, from potency of the subjacent (i.e. by causing a subjacent matter to pass from potency to act).'

'true growths': the appearance of life, of a 'metaphysical species', of each human soul.

This concept obviously comes up against all sorts of historical improbabilities and intellectual incompatibilities.

a. It obliges us to see, between the successive degrees of being (physical, organic, spiritual) which are so obviously linked in their *appearance*, no more than a logical connexion, a purely intellectual plan which has artificially disposed beings in an appearance of continuity.

b. In consequence, it makes it impossible to explain the physical interdependence (in their *functioning*) which we observe in the various organs of the universe. And yet it is quite obvious that thought must have a certain organic support, which is itself a function of certain physico-chemical conditions.

c. Finally, it denies any absolute value to the work of secondary causes: they no longer have any organic effectiveness in causing the world to pass through the different levels of being.

It appears to me that most of the difficulties presented to Scholasticism by the historical evidence of evolution derive from the failure to consider (in addition to creation and eduction) a third sort of perfectly well-defined movement: *creative transformation*.

Beside '*creatio ex nihilo subjecti*' and '*transformatio ex potentia subjecti*',[3] there is room for an act *sui generis* which *makes use* of a pre-existent created being and builds it up into a *completely new being*.

This *act is really creative*, because it calls for renewed intervention on the part of the First Cause.

And at the same time it *depends upon a subject* (a subjacent) – on *something in a subject*.

It is most remarkable that Scholasticism has no word to designate this method of divine operation which:

3. See notes 1 and 2 above.

a. is conceivable *in abstracto*, and is therefore entitled to a place at least in speculation,

b. is probably the only one which satisfies our experience of the world.

We should, I believe, have to be blind not to see this: *In natura rerum* (in nature) the two categories of movement separated by Scholasticism (*Creatio et Eductio*) are seen to be constantly fused, combined, together.

There is not one moment when God creates, and one moment when the secondary causes develop. There is always only *one* creative action (identical with conservation) which continually raises creatures towards fuller-being, *by means of* their secondary activity and their earlier advances.

Understood in this way, creation is not a periodic intrusion of the First Cause: it is an act co-extensive with the whole duration of the universe. God *has been creating* ever since the beginning of time, and, *seen from within*, his creation (*even his initial creation?*) takes the form of a transformation. Participated being is not introduced *in batches* which are differentiated later as a result of a non-creative modification: God is continually breathing new being into us.

All along the curve followed by being in its augmentations there are, of course, levels, particular points, at which creative action becomes dominant (the appearance of life and of thought).

Strictly speaking, however, *every* good movement is, in some of its content, creative.

With creation continuing incessantly as a function of all that already exists, there is *never*, properly speaking, any '*nihilum subjecti*' (nothingness of subjacent matter) – *apart from so considering the universe in its total formation throughout the ages*.

This notion of 'creative transformation' (or creation by transformation) which I have just been analysing seems to me to be impregnable in itself, and the only notion that fits in with the world of our experience. What is more, it brings real 'emancipation': it puts an end to the paradox and the stumbling-block of matter (i.e. our bewilderment when we consider the part played by the brain in thought and by passion – ἔρως[4] – in mysticism); and it transforms them both into a noble and illuminated cult of that same matter.

If it is a fact, as it seems to me, that 'creative transformation' is a concept which as yet has no place in Scholasticism, then I think that it should be introduced without delay, and so prevent the orthodox *theological* notion of creation from being any longer stifled and distorted by the '*nihilum subjecti*' of one particular philosophy.

Unpublished, no date. Probably written at the beginning of 1920.

4. Eros, the love which desires, as opposed to agape, the love which gives.

NOTE ON THE
MODES OF DIVINE ACTION
IN THE UNIVERSE

A COMPARISON may help to bring home in a more concrete form the reflections that follow. Imagine a sphere, and within it a large number of springs packed close together. Let these springs, moreover, be free to expand or contract as they wish, spontaneously. Such a system may represent the universe and the multitude of activities, all part and parcel of one another, which make it up.

Supposing now that inside this mechanical model of the world we try to represent by some device the influence of the First Cause. What element should we add or what modification could we impose on the parts contained in the sphere, to symbolize God's intervention in secondary causes?

A first way of introducing the 'God' factor into our system that represents the world would be to add an *extra spring*, much more central and more powerful than all the others, to the assembly of living springs contained in the sphere, which would make them conform to its will. There would be a God-spring, just as there is a Peter-spring or a Paul-spring, and so on. A dominant causality *among* the other causalities (in short, a force interpolated into the series of experiential forces) – that is what the divine influence would be.

Often though so rudimentary a way of understanding God's operative activity in the universe is, more or less unconsciously, accepted, we obviously cannot take it as it stands. The purpose of this note is to emphasize the fact that the only rational ways in which we can conceive the Creator's action on his works are those which oblige us to regard the introduction into things of the divine energy as *being* (from the experiential point of view) *imperceptible*: a property which cannot but have important consequences bearing on these two questions:

How is God knowable to us? (Part I)

What is the true extension (in the logical sense) of his omnipotence? (Part II)

I

a. A first, and peculiarly divine, way by which the First Cause can affect lower natures consists in its ability to act *simultaneously on their whole body*. To go back to our sphere of springs, we may imagine outside it a being capable of exerting so skilful a pressure over the whole of the surface of the system at once that it can, infallibly, produce whatever modification it wishes at any point inside the sphere. Let us suppose that such a modification is being produced. From the point of view of the springs situated at the point affected, the external (= creative) impulse will come from every direction and will appear to be either the result of pure coincidence or the effect of a mysterious force operating throughout the whole of the inside of the sphere. It is impossible to localize the new energy introduced into the system: it has all the appearance of a chance or an immanence.[1] This is how (from the strictly experiential point of view) we see the influence of Providence on the world. We cannot pin down the point at which the hand of God is apparent. It acts upon the whole body of causes without making itself evident at any point: thus, externally, there is nothing so like the action of the Prime Mover as the action of a soul of the world, so much like the divine wisdom as destiny or

---

1. If the comparison is to be more exact, we must, it is clear, assume that the sphere has an infinite radius, and that the transmission of the 'external' force is effected *instantaneously* (each element being *simultaneously* influenced *as a function* of *all the others*). (Note by Père Teilhard.)

fate. It would be beside the point to wonder whether such an arrangement suits us or not: *it is there*, and that is all about it.

b. Even though every individual action is integral with the general state and overall modifications of the whole, in essence the individual represents an autonomous centre of operation. The divine action, therefore, cannot limit itself to enclosing and moulding individual natures from outside. In order fully to dominate them, it must have a hold on their innermost life. Hence, in addition to the faculty of acting *upon the whole at once*, the First Cause must be able to make itself felt at the core of each element of the world individually. A moment ago we were considering a being so external to things that it embraced them all together in its influence. Now let us imagine the same being become so interior to the springs it controls that it can, as it wishes, increase or relax their tension up to the extreme limit of their elasticity (actual or potential). In that image we shall have produced a more or less accurate picture of God's *particular* operation, that by which he controls the world, not simply as a whole, but as an assembly of *individually vitalized* beings. In this case, the action of the transcendent Cause is perfectly localized. It intervenes at a very precisely determined point in the universe. Does that mean that we may perhaps be able to apprehend it? By no means: in this case, again, the divine operation appears only 'at the level of the rest', as an immediately discernible element. By reason of its extreme interiority it becomes inapprehensible. The spring, moved *ab intra* – from within – by the being animating the sphere, can perfectly well imagine that it is acting alone (whereas *it is being acted upon*), and the other springs, its neighbours, share the illusion. This is what happens in the field of our experience. Where God is operating it is always possible for us (by remaining at a certain level) to see only the *work of nature*.

Thus, sometimes by *excess of extension*, sometimes by *excess of depth*, the point at which the divine force is applied is essentially extra-phenomenal. The First Cause is not involved in effects; it acts upon individual *natures* and on the movement of *the whole*. Properly speaking, God *does not make*: He *makes things make themselves*. That is why there is no breach or cleavage at the point at which he enters. The network of determinisms remains intact – the harmony of organic developments continues without discord. And yet the Master has entered into his own.

But, it will be objected, if the condition of the divine action is that it is always shrouded in chance, in determinism, in immanence, then we are obliged to admit that the divine causality is not *directly* apprehensible – either as creative in the movement which orders the world, or as revealing in the miracle.

That is perfectly true.

Whether it be ordinary Providence, or miraculous Providence (extraordinary coincidences), or even, again, the prodigy (θαῦμα), *we shall never be enabled scientifically* to see God, because there will never be any discontinuity between the divine operation and the physical and physiological laws which are science's sole concern. Since the chains of antecedents are never broken (but simply bent or extended) by divine action, an analytical observation of phenomena is powerless to enable us to attain God, *even as Prime Mover*. We shall never escape *scientifically* from the circle of natural explanations. This is something which we simply have to accept.

This property in the Divine of being inapprehensible to any material grasp has always been emphasized in connexion with the miraculous. Except for the cases of the restoration of life to the dead (which are extremely rare and, apart from those recorded in the Gospels, all more or less arguable) there are, in the history of the Church, no miracles that cannot be explained by vital forces that have been remarkably augmented *in their own direction*. On the other hand, we have no example (even in legend) of a 'morphological' miracle[2] – nor has it ever been recorded that a martyr emerged from the fire and survived the sword.

We may be quite certain, then, that the more miracles are studied medically, the more (after a first phase of astonishment) *they will be found to be extensions* of biology – just as the more the past of the universe and of mankind is studied scientifically, the more we find evidence of an evolution.

And yet, God is knowable by human reason. And yet, the miracle is absolutely necessary, not only because it is needed in apologetics, but also for the joy it brings to our hearts: the heart cannot find complete rest in a God whom it does not feel to be stronger than anything that exists.

How are we to succeed in apprehending the presence of the divine current beneath the continuous web of phenomena – the creative transcendence through evolutive immanence?

It is here that we have to introduce those useful theories which develop to its fullest extent, in the matter of intellectual knowledge, the system of act and potency, and so recognize in the faculties of the soul the power to *attain the full truth* about the objects they perceive.

Without any doubt, there lies hidden beneath the ascending movement of life, the continuous action of a being who raises up the universe from within. Beneath the uninterrupted operation of secondary causes, there is produced (in many miracles) an exceptional expansion of natures, much greater than could result from the normal functioning of created factors and stimuli. Considered objectively, material facts *have in them something of the Divine*. In relation, however, to our knowledge, this divine element in them is no more than a potency. It will remain *in potency* so long as we lack, for actualizing in our mind the supra-sensible world, faculties that are sufficiently trained; and the training must come not only from the practice of

2. E.g. the restoration of a limb. (Note by Père Teilhard.)

analysis and criticism but, much more, from a sharpening of moral sensibility, and a complete loyalty in following the ever-rising star of truth. Only *purity of heart* (assisted or not by grace, as the case may be) *and not pure science* is capable, confronted by the world in movement or by a miraculous fact, of overcoming the essential indeterminacy of appearances and of unmistakably disclosing a creator behind the forces of nature – and the Divine underlying the abnormal.

Already, then, we see that the study of the conditions imposed on the divine operation by the nature of the world, obliges us to adopt a particular theory of the knowledge of God (knowledge by reason and knowledge by faith).[3] We now have to see how the existence of such conditions, which apparently impose limitations upon the Prime Causality, can be reconciled with an unimpeachable view of divine omnipotence.

II

In deciding whether or not beings are qualified to exist, we have become accustomed to considering only one type of possibility in them – *logical possibility* – in other words the internal non-contradiction of the abstract concepts by which we define their natures. Man, for example, is considered possible because 'animality' is not incompatible with 'rationality'. In consequence, man is said to be actualizable *simpliciter* (purely and simply) by the divine power; and, once that has been granted, there is no longer any need, we would say, to ask whether this

3. It will be noted that the considerations developed above in connexion with the *scientific invisibility* of divine causality (even in the miraculous) are the necessary counterpart of every theory which requires, for apperception of the Divine, a particular sensitizing of the faculties of the soul. Without some inherent natural ambiguity in the *objective* aspect of miraculous facts, it would be impossible to explain the fact that, *subjectively*, we need 'eyes of faith' to recognize the hand of God. (Note by Père Teilhard.)

actualizing of a 'possible' does not itself have *its own conditions of possibility*. In the eyes of many philosophers, the universe holds together solely through the intelligibility of its elements, considered in isolation and fully formed. The questions of becoming and of the whole do not exist for such thinkers, so that, as they see it, there is no reason for doubting that God, if he so wished, could bring into existence 'from scratch' – *ex nihilo sui et subjecti, et mundi recipientis* (without pre-existence of self or subjacent, or of world to receive them) – Peter or Paul, completely alone and completely sanctified. That is what is constantly said or assumed in the Schools.

Very well, then; if we are to give full freedom to the truth, there is something we must have the courage to say about such an estimate of the creative power. It consists in taking only two or three terms in the interminable series of ontological conditions to which our being is subject, and putting them together as though they were interchangeable pieces; this is not only puerile, it belittles both God and ourselves – not to mention that it gives rise to the most serious difficulties in connexion with Providence.

In so far as we can judge the progress of the world, God's power has not so free a field for its action as we assume: on the contrary, in virtue of the very constitution of the participated being it labours to produce (that is, briefly, in virtue of the perfection proper to itself), it is always obliged, in the course of its creative effort, to pass through a whole series of intermediaries and to overcome a whole succession of inevitable risks – whatever may be said by the theologians, who are always ready to introduce the operation of the '*potentia absoluta divina*' (the absolute power of God).

We have already recognized a first very general law to which God's operation is subject *ad extra* (in so far as it operates outside itself): that, precisely in virtue of its own perfection, it is unable to act in discontinuity with individual natures or out of harmony with the advance of the whole – that is, it must operate on the same plane as the secondary causes. This first restriction on the 'arbitrary' manifestation of God's action leads us to a consideration of two more.

1. First of all, it appears contradictory (to the nature of participated being) to imagine God creating an *isolated* thing. Only one being can exist in isolation: *Ens a se* (Being which exists only in itself). Everything which is not God is essentially multitude – multitude organized in itself, and multitude organizing around itself. If God, then, is to *make a soul*, there is only one way open to his power: *to create a world*.[4] In consequence, man includes among his fully realized conditions of possibility more than just 'animality and rationality'; the notion of man implies also 'mankind, earth, universe. . . .' This takes us a long way from the facile 'possibility' which the logicians imagine for things. But at the same time it adds to our stature – and, most of all, when applied to our Lord, it suggests the idea of an astonishing unity in creation. For now at last we can see that if God wished to have Christ, to launch a complete universe and scatter life with a lavish hand was no more than he was obliged to do. Strictly speaking, then, is there, in all that moves outside God, anything else *in act* today, other than the actualizing of Jesus Christ, for which each fragment of the world is, proximately or distantly, necessary (*ex necessitate medii* – as a necessary means)? We need have no hesitation in saying that there is not.

2. If the general laws of becoming (controlling the progressive

---

4. *A world*, i.e. not only a *whole*, but a *progressive* whole. We are inclined to conceive the power of God as supremely uninhibited in the face of 'non-being'. In this we are mistaken. '*Non-being*' *offers God only an infinitesimal purchase-point* (obediental potentiality); God, therefore, can overcome it only *gradatim* (gradually), by producing participated being which is progressively more capable of supporting the creative effort. This is what makes itself apparent to us as an evolution. (Note by Père Teilhard.)

appearance of being – created being – from an unorganized multiple) must be regarded as modalities rigorously imposed on God's action, then we can begin to see that *the existence of evil* might very well also be a *strictly inevitable* concomitant of the creation. '*Necesse est ut adveniant scandala.*'[5]

We often represent God to ourselves as being able to draw from non-being a world without sorrows, faults, dangers – a world in which there is no damage, no breakage. This is a conceptual fantasy, and makes it impossible to solve the problem of evil.

No, we have to accept that in spite of his power God *cannot* obtain a creature united to himself without necessarily engaging in a struggle with some evil. For evil appears *inevitably* with the first atom of being which creation 'releases' into existence. Creature and sinlessness (absolute and general) are terms whose association is as incompatible (whether physically or metaphysically is of little moment here) with God's power and wisdom as the coupling of 'creature' and 'oneness'. In consequence if evil is rampant all around us on earth, we should not be shocked but rather hold up our heads in pride. These tears, this blood, and these vices, are in reality a measure of the value that we represent. Our being must, indeed, be precious for God to continue to seek it through so many obstacles. And it is a great honour that he makes us able to fight with him, 'that his word may be accomplished' – in other words that 'there may be creature'.

We see, then, that the old idea of fate which ruled even the gods was not completely false. No one has ever thought it remarkable that God cannot make a square circle or perform an evil act. Why should we restrict the field of impossible contradiction only to those cases? There are certainly *physical* equivalents to the inflexible laws of moral science and geometry.

5. 'For it is necessary that temptations come' (Matthew 18:7). The exact wording of the Vulgate is, '*Necesse est enim ut veniant scandala*'.

In what form, then, are we ultimately to conceive the necessary and eminently desirable omnipotence of God? If God is in truth obliged (by a necessity immanent in himself), when he wishes to create, to work through certain laws of development, how can the ultimate decision lie in his creative act? By what miracle will the Creator govern things: will it not be things that are in control of him?

The answer to this final question must be: 'By the supreme miracle of the divine power, which consists in being able, through a deep-reaching and all-embracing influence, incessantly to *integrate*, on a higher plane, all good and all evil in the reality which that power builds up by means of secondary causes.' To return once more, and finally, to the comparison of the sphere filled with living springs: at every moment the spontaneous activity of the springs tends to modify and upset the equilibrium sought by the dominant being we have imagined as in charge of their assembly. Let us assume that this being is able constantly to use the new state produced in the system and refashion it: that he can make the continually new disposition of the elements of the sphere serve his ends so well that throughout all the fluctuations and in spite of all the resistance his design meets (or more exactly, *by means* of them), it continues without interruption. This assumption will give us a good enough picture of God's action, at once *imperceptible* and *irresistible*, on the progress of events.

All of us in this world are caught up in a tangle of evils and determinisms upon which God himself (in virtue of his freely asserted creative act) can act only under certain very precise conditions – and this because there are 'obstructions' which are *essentially* part of things. Yet, even if the threads are unbreakable or elastic only up to a point, the fabric itself is infinitely supple in the hands of the Creator – provided that we, on our side, show ourselves to be faithful creatures. Let man live at a distance from God, and the universe remains neutral or hostile to him. But let man believe in God, and immediately all around him the elements, even the irksome, of the inevitable organize themselves into a friendly whole, ordered to the ultimate success of life. For the believer everything is still, externally and individually, what it is for all the world; and yet God's power solicitously adapts the whole to serve him. At every moment it in some way re-creates the universe expressly for the man who prays to it. '*Credenti omnia convertuntur in bonum.*'[6]

An infallible synthesis of the whole, operated by combined internal and external influences; such, in brief, would appear to be (apart from the exceptional amplifications we meet in miracles) the most general and most perfected form of God's action upon the world: respecting all, 'forced into' many roundabout ways and obliged to tolerate many things which shock us at first – but ultimately integrating and transforming all.

Unpublished, January 1920.

6. This amounts to saying that God exercises an overall activity in the universe (providence), which cannot be reduced to, though it is co-extensive with, the sum total of elementary activities into which our experience analyses it (breaks it down). (Note by Père Teilhard.)

Credenti . . . bonum: For the believer all things are converted into good.

FALL, REDEMPTION, AND GEOCENTRISM

THE principal obstacle encountered by orthodox thinkers when they try to accommodate the *revealed* historical picture of human origins to the present scientific evidence, is the traditional notion of original sin. It is the Pauline theory of the Fall and the two Adams which (somewhat illogically, we may add) makes it impossible to regard all the details found in Genesis as equally didactic and symbolic. It is that theory which is responsible for the jealous maintenance, as a dogma, of strict monogenism (first one man, and then one man and one woman), which it is in actual fact impossible for science to accept.

It should be borne in mind that those prehistorians who share the Christian faith have good reason to anticipate a revision in their favour of exegetical and dogmatic intransigence in this connexion. It is not only, in fact, a few palaeontological discoveries which are forcing the Church to lose no time in modifying her ideas about the *historical evidence* of human origins. The whole new physiognomy of the universe, as disclosed to us for some centuries now, is introducing an intrinsic imbalance into the very core of the dogma; and we cannot escape from this except through an extensive metamorphosis of the notion of original sin.

As a result of the collapse of geocentrism, which she has come to accept, the Church is now caught between her historico-dogmatic representation of the world's origin, on the one hand, and the requirements of one of her most fundamental dogmas on the other – so that she cannot retain the former without to some degree sacrificing the latter.

This is the point that I now want to make clear.

———

The historico-dogmatic representation of things I am speaking of, is the conviction that evil (first moral, and then physical) entered the world as the result of *a fault* committed by an *individual human being*.

The fundamental dogma is the *universality* of the corruption let loose by the initial human fault. The *whole* universe, the faithful believe, was perverted by Adam's disobedience; and it is *because* of that universal perversion that the Redemption, in turn, was extended to the entire universe, and that Christ became the centre of the neo-creation.

In earlier times, until Galileo,[1] there was perfect compatibility between historical representation of the Fall and dogma of universal redemption – and all the more easily, too, in that each was modelled on the other.[2] So long as people believed, as St Paul himself did, in one week of creation and a past of 4,000 years – so long as people thought the stars were satellites of the earth, and that animals were there to serve man – there was no difficulty in believing that a single man could

1. We are astonished, or simply smile, at the anxiety the Church experienced when she first came up against Galileo's system. In fact, the theologians of the time were quite correct in their *presentiment*. With the end of geocentrism, what was emerging was the evolutionist point of view. All that Galileo's judges could distinctly see as menaced was the miracle of Joshua. The fact was that in consequence the seeds of decomposition had been introduced into the whole of the Genesis theory of the Fall: and we are only today beginning to appreciate the depth of the changes which at that time were already potentially completed. (Note by Père Teilhard.)

2. It is interesting to note that if (in the case of original sin) we suffer from an internal conflict between our dogmatic history and our beliefs, it is because the *former has introduced a dogma which it can no longer justify*. Our dogma tends to hold on *sua mole* – by its own mass – *independently of the value of the historical concepts which produced it!* (=it 'explodes' them). (Note by Père Teilhard.)

37

have ruined everything, and that another man had saved everything.

Today we know, with absolute physical certainty, that the stellar universe is not centred on the earth, and that terrestrial life is not centred on mankind. The movement which carries us along takes the form not of a divergence from a lower cosmic centre, but rather of a slow concentration, in all orders, from layers of extreme diffusion; and even if an initial centre of the world does exist, we certainly cannot locate it among human beings. Thousands of centuries before a thinking being appeared on our earth, life swarmed on it, with its instincts and its passions, its sufferings and its deaths. And it is almost impossible to conceive that, among the millions of Milky Ways which whirl in space, there is not one which has known, or is going to know, conscious life – and that evil, the same evil as that which is such a blemish on earth, is not contaminating all of them, like some most insidious ether.

A believer who examines the horizons opened up by such considerations, realizes that he is caught in a dilemma:

Either he must completely redraw the historical representation of original sin (= a first man's disobedience);

Or he must restrict the theological Fall and Redemption to a small portion of the universe that has reached such boundless dimensions. The Bible, St Paul, Christ, the Virgin and so on, would hold good only for earth. Whenever Scripture speaks of 'world' we would have to understand 'earth' – and, more particularly, 'mankind' – and more particularly still, maybe, that particular branch of mankind which emerged from an individual called Adam.

I am well aware that some Thomist theologians will not shrink from the second of these alternatives. They will prefer a restricted conception of the Fall and Redemption at the cost, in spite of its danger, of modifying an historical edifice closely bound up with dogmas grafted on to it.

And yet I know, too, that these same thinkers are abandoning the substance of dogma and tradition for a hollow shell. They can defend their positions verbally, but they have lost the truth. The *spirit* of the Bible and the Church is perfectly clear: the *whole* world has been corrupted by the Fall and the *whole* of everything has been redeemed. Christ's glory, beauty, and irresistible attraction radiate, in short, from his *universal* kingship. If his dominance is restricted to the sublunary regions, then he is eclipsed, he is abjectly extinguished by the universe. *'Qui descendit, nisi qui ascendit, ut repleret omnia?'*[3]

The Church cannot measure up to the truth except by universalizing the first and the second Adam.

I. THE FIRST ADAM

Let me say frankly what I think: it is impossible to universalize the first Adam without destroying his individuality. Even if we conceive mankind as *'singularis'* or *'unica'*[4] (a point we shall be discussing later),[5] we can no longer derive the whole of evil from one single hominian. I must emphasize again that long before man death existed on earth. And in the depths of the heavens, far from any moral influence of the earth, death also exists. Now, St Paul is categorical: *'Per peccatum mors.'*[6] Sin (original sin) does not explain the suffering and the mor-

3. Eph. 4:10: 'He who descended is he who also ascended . . . that he might fill all things.'

4. 'Singular' in the philosophical sense of the word, alone of its kind, unique.

5. In thus denying the historicity of 'Adam' Père Teilhard is not for all that denying the essence of the dogma of original sin, which is the universality of sin in every man, with, in consequence, the necessity of universal redemption. For the present theological attitude to these extremely complex problems, see *Le Dogme du péché originel*, by Père Charles Baumgartner, s.j. (Desclée et Cie, Paris, 1969).

6. 'Death [comes] through sin.' Cf. Romans 5:12.

tality only of man: for St Paul it explains all suffering. *It is the general solution of the problem of evil.*[7]

Since, in the universe we know today, neither one man nor the whole of mankind can be responsible for contaminating the whole, we must (if we are to retain what is essential in St Paul's thought) remove from his language what represents the expression of the ideas of a first-century Jew – instead of trying to preserve precisely those outdated formulations at the expense of the apostle's fundamental faith.

I would not be so foolish as to point out to the Church her proper line of advance; but when, for my own personal satisfaction, I explore the possible ways out from the difficulty, I believe that I can see daylight along these lines: original sin, taken in its widest sense, is not a malady specific to the earth, nor is it bound up with human generation. It simply symbolizes the inevitable chance of evil (*Necesse est ut eveniant scandala*)[8] which accompanies the existence of all participated being. Wherever being *in fieri*[9] is produced, suffering and wrong immediately appear as its shadow: not only as a result of the tendency towards inaction and selfishness found in creatures, but also (which is more disturbing) as an inevitable concomitant of their effort to progress. Original sin is the essential reaction of the finite to the creative act. Inevitably it insinuates itself into existence through the medium of all creation. It is the *reverse side* of all creation. By the very fact that he creates, God commits himself to a fight against evil and in consequence to, in one way or another, effecting a redemption. The

7. To admit that there is, anywhere at all, suffering without sin, is to run counter to the thought of St Paul. For St Paul, original sin is so full an explanation of death that the existence of death is in itself sufficient to justify the deduction that there has been sin. I realize that Thomist theologians do not accept this, even though they claim the support of St Paul for their view. (Note by Père Teilhard.)

8. 'It must be that scandals come.'   9. 'In process of becoming.'

specifically human Fall is no more than the (broadly speaking, collective and eternal) actualizing of this '*fomes peccati*'[10] which was infused, long before us, into the whole of the universe, from the lowest zones of matter to the angelic spheres. Strictly speaking, there is no first Adam. The name disguises a universal and unbreakable law of reversion or perversion – the price that has to be paid for progress.[11]

II. THE SECOND ADAM

The case of the second Adam is completely different. There is, it is clear, no lower centre of divergence in the universe at which we could place the first Adam. On the contrary – the universe can and must be conceived as converging towards a point of supreme confluence. In virtue, moreover, of its universal and increasing unification, it possesses this property, that each of its elements is organically connected with all the others. In these circumstances, there is nothing to prevent a human individual nature from having been so chosen, and its omni-influence having been so elevated, that from being '*una inter pares*'[12] it has become '*prima super omnes*'.[13] Just as in living bodies a cell, at first similar to the other cells, can gradually come to be preponderant in the organism, so the particular humanity of Christ was able (at least at the Resurrection) to take on, to acquire, a universal morphological function. Unlike what we found in the case of the first Adam, the universality

10. Literally, 'kindling, touchwood' – stimulus to, pabulum of, sin.

11. According to this hypothesis, moral evil is indeed (as St Paul holds) bound up with physical evil, but in virtue of an immanent sanction, the latter being a necessary accompaniment of the former. Progress-creation, transgression-fall, suffering-redemption, are three physically inseparable terms, which mutually counterbalance and vindicate one another – and the *three must be taken together as one* if we are fully to understand *the meaning of the Cross*. (Note by Père Teilhard.)

12. 'One among its equals.'   13. 'First above all.'

of action possessed by a personal Christ is both understandable and eminently satisfying *in se*.[14] There is, however, a difficulty; how to make this universal action intellectually *convincing* in the face of the limitless cosmos which experience is now revealing to us. How are we to explain the astonishing coincidence which, in spite of the vastness of the ether and duration, has made us live – within a few years – at the same time as the Redeemer and on the same speck of stellar dust? And how are we to conceive the form taken in other domains of the cosmos by this Redemption which has been effected in an imperceptibly small area of time and space?

I must admit that when the intellect has to face these problems there is a strong temptation to fall back on a qualified geocentrism. Why not admit that earth is the only point of spiritual liberation in this boundless universe? The depths of the firmament should not cause us to lose heart. Spirit is born at the surface which separates two cosmic spheres, which are, roughly speaking, the spheres of molecules and of stars. Just as below us, in our *inner body*, analysis shows us how corpuscles continue to multiply in countless thousands – so, too, above us, in our *outer body*, nebulae jostle one another in millions: their myriads at all times form but one body, our own. We must, it is true, abandon the idea of a universe initially derived from a single man; but we can still, perhaps, believe in a universe the whole of whose conscious forces have no other point of precipitation, no other point of release, but the human brain. And in that case the head of humankind, Christ, would be placed directly at the psychic pole of creation: he would immediately be universalized.

If it seems really too anthropocentric to imagine a *unique* mankind in the universe, we can still fall back on conceiving it as only singular (*singularis*). Among all the centres of consciousness that are or can be realized in the world, we represent per-

14. 'In itself.'

haps the most central, or the lowest, or the most culpable . . . Above us, we know, lie the angelic series; and, in spite of what the Schoolmen say when they treat the nature of pure spirits as they would a geometric construction, they are continuous with our material world. We are in some way the lower term of those series, the link which provides a direct connexion with the multiple and the unconscious. Since men occupy this humble but special position, it is understandable that in order to reach all things the universal Redeemer should have entered among us – introducing himself into the lowest of the spiritual spheres, precisely '*ut repleret omnia*'.[15]

If the earth may be conceived as '*unica*', or at least as '*singularis*' *in natura rerum*,[16] then our co-existence in time and space with Christ is no more extraordinary than our own personal co-existence with the earth and the present. The new Adam was made man, rather than anything else, for a reason intrinsic to mankind.

That may be perfectly true; but the whole problem is to find out whether in order to retain this supreme geocentrism, so comforting a concession to our weakness, we are not obliged to resist the truth. A mankind which proclaims that it is alone, or in a special position, in the universe reminds us of the philosopher who claims to reduce the whole of the real to his own consciousness, so exclusively as to deny true existence to other men. It is an undoubted fact that *to achieve the proper balance of a single soul* calls for as many nebulae in the depths of the heavens as there are molecules in the heart of matter. But just as the human soul is not alone, but essentially legion, on the surface of the earth, so it is infinitely probable that the conscious layer of the cosmos is not confined to a single point (our mankind) but continues beyond the earth into other stars and other times. *In all probability* mankind is neither '*unica*' nor

15. 'That he might fill all things' (Eph. 4:10).
16. 'Unique' or 'singular' in nature.

'*singularis*', but is 'one among a thousand'. How, then, is it that, against all probability, this particular mankind was chosen as the centre of the Redemption? And how, from that starting-point, can Redemption be extended from star to star?

As far as I can see, this question is still unanswered. The idea of an earth chosen *arbitrarily* from countless others as the focus of Redemption is one that I cannot accept; and on the other hand the hypothesis of a special revelation, in some millions of centuries to come, teaching the inhabitants of the system of Andromeda that the Word was incarnate on earth, is just ridiculous. All that I can entertain is the possibility of a multi-aspect Redemption which would be realized, as one and the same Redemption, on all the stars – rather as the sacrifice of the mass is multiplied, still the same sacrifice, at all times and in all places. Yet all the worlds do not coincide in time! There were worlds before our own, and there will be other worlds after it . . . Unless we introduced a relativity into time we should have to admit, surely, that Christ has still to be incarnate in some as yet unformed star? . . . And what, then, becomes of '*Christus iam non moritur*'?[17] And what becomes, too, of the unique role of the Virgin Mary?

There are times when one almost despairs of being able to disentangle Catholic dogmas from the geocentrism in the framework of which they were born. And yet one thing in the Catholic creed is more certain than anything: that there is a Christ '*in quo omnia constant*'.[18] All secondary beliefs will have to give way, if necessary, to this fundamental article. Christ is all or nothing.

Unpublished, 20 July 1920.

17. 'Christ being raised from the dead will never die again' (Romans 6:9).
18. 'In whom all things hold together' (Col. 1:17).

NOTE ON SOME POSSIBLE
HISTORICAL REPRESENTATIONS
OF ORIGINAL SIN

IN speaking of original sin there are two things which we should carefully distinguish:

1. The dogmatic attributes of the first transgression (the universal necessity of Redemption, *fomes peccati*,[1] etc.).

2. The external circumstances in which this transgression was committed: by that I mean the outward forms it has assumed, its representation.

Hitherto (apart from the school of Alexandria) the representation of original sin has been borrowed almost literally from the first chapters of Genesis. It is apparent that today we are being irresistibly driven to find a new way of picturing to ourselves the events as a consequence of which evil invaded our world. The aim of this note is:

1. To show as a result of what findings Christian thought is being gradually obliged to abandon its former ways of conceiving original sin.

2. To indicate certain directions in which believers would now appear to be turning in their attempt to present the dogma of the Fall in a way that can be reconciled with what is least hypothetical in the evidence of experience and history.

I. DIFFICULTIES IN THE TRADITIONAL REPRESENTATION

There is a twofold and serious difficulty in retaining the former representation of original sin. It may be expressed as follows: 'The more we bring the past to life again by means of science,

1. See note, p. 41.

the less we can accommodate either Adam or the earthly paradise.'

1. *No acceptable place for Adam.* Zoologists are practically unanimous in admitting a true unity of the human race. Nevertheless, we should be careful to note that they attach to this unity a meaning very different from the monogenism of the theologians. As natural scientists see it, mankind probably emerged from one and the same animal group. Its appearance, however, must have been gradual, through a number of avenues and perhaps through a number of channels of transmission. The stem by which the human species is attached to the common main trunk of living beings must, in fact, be sufficiently complex to contain 'in potency' the great varieties of human types known to us. This presupposes its having a section (a numerical base) of considerable width, and considerable shading-off at its edges. If we try to concentrate in one single individual (or one single pair) all the primitive characteristics that can be recognized in Heidelberg man, Neanderthal man, the Tasmanians, Australians, etc., we arrive at an extremely dehumanized being, maybe a monstrosity. In any case (and quite apart from the extreme improbability of the realization of a zoological type in one individual) such a procedure gives us an Adam most ill-adapted to bearing in himself the complete responsibilities of our race.

2. *Still less place, in our historical picture, for the earthly paradise.* The earthly paradise can no longer be understood in these days as a specially favoured reservation of some few acres. We now see that everything in the universe holds together physically, chemically, and zoologically, too integrally for the *permanent* absence of death, suffering and evil (even for a small fraction of things) to be conceivable outside a *general state* of the world different from our own. The earthly paradise is intelligible only

as a *different way of being* for the universe (which fits in with the traditional meaning of the dogma, which sees in Eden 'another world'). Yet, however far back we look into the past we find nothing that resembles this wonderful state. There is not the least trace on the horizon, not the smallest scar, to mark the ruins of a golden age or our cutting off from a better world. As far as the mind can reach, looking backwards, we find the world dominated by physical evil, impregnated with moral evil (sin is manifestly 'in potency' close to actuality as soon as the least spontaneity appears) – we find it *in a state of original sin.*

The truth is that it is so impossible to include Adam and the earthly paradise (taken literally) in our scientific outlook, that I wonder whether a single person today can *at the same time* focus his mind on the geological world presented by science, and on the world commonly described by sacred history. We cannot retain both pictures without moving alternately from one to the other. Their association clashes, it rings false. In combining them on one and the same plane we are certainly victims of an error in perspective.

II. NEW POSSIBLE WAYS OF CONCEIVING ORIGINAL SIN

Since there is no room in the scientific history of the world for the point at which original sin marks a retrogression; since, in the series *known to our experience*, everything happens as though there were no Adam and no Eden; then it must be that the Fall, as an event, is something which cannot be verified or checked. For some reason the traces of the initial tragedy necessarily escape our analysis of the world. This characteristic of being impatient of verification can derive from two completely opposite causes:

1. Either original sin is an event which escapes us because it is too small and distant;

2. Or, the contrary is true: we cannot distinguish it because it is too big and too close to us in time.

A. Conservative theologians seem to me to concentrate on the first alternative and try to reconcile the Bible and science. All along the line, they minimize. Today, the preternatural gifts given to our first parents are whittled down as far as possible. The range of the properties found in the earthly paradise is reduced. The consequences of the transgression are limited by saying that the 'suffering and death introduced into the world' simply refers to man's suffering and death (which is manifestly contrary to the spirit – if not to the letter – of St Paul, for whom the Fall is above all a solution to the problem of evil). This first way of solving the problem of its being impossible to pin down original sin is both precarious and humiliating. It avoids criticism by simply giving up; and, what is more serious, it compromises the very content of the dogma. If the era of paradise has made so feeble a physical impact on the historical progress of the world, how can we reasonably expect it to bear the weight of the new earth and the new heavens?

We must look for the solution of our problem in the opposite direction. The reason why original sin eludes our detection is not because its smallness baffles it but because its very magnitude transcends it.

B. How are we to conceive this transcendence of original sin in relation to our experience? Let me give various ways in which this may be done.

a. A first possible explanation (the most conservative and the most 'realist') of the 'unverifiable' character of the very opening stages of mankind's history is to introduce the symbol of a new *switch* of the human world, which occurred as a consequence of original sin. On this hypothesis we shall say that Adam and Eve began their existence in a sphere of the world different from ours. Through their fall they sank into a lower sphere (now our own); in other words they were embodied as matter in, incarnated in, fitted into, the strictly animal sphere into which we are now born: they were *reborn* at a lower level than that of their first state. Having, therefore, followed a by-road until it brought them to the road represented by the terrestrial universe, they lost sight (as we, too, have done) of the place from which they came, and of the road which had led them to their position 'among the beasts'. Like travellers who have turned sharp to the right at a circular clearing in a forest, we no longer realize which path our race has in fact been following; but behind us we can see receding into infinity

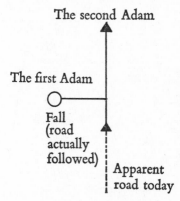

The second Adam

The first Adam

Fall
(road
actually
followed)

Apparent
road today

the zoological series into which we were belatedly incorporated. This satisfactorily explains our inability to distinguish in the past the least trace of an earthly paradise. To avoid the difficulties of strict monogenism, we should have to add either that Adam and Eve symbolize the origin of mankind, or else that their downfall in some way pluralized them (dissociated them, disintegrated them) to the extent required by their natural in clusion in an evolutive animal series (such series being made up of groups of beings, not from a single pair of individuals).

b. Following this first explanation, there is some difficulty in conceiving the animal world, evolving on its own, into

49

which our first parents would have sunk. Logically, the idea of a 'bifurcation' and 'switch' in the initial human world suggests that it should be carried through to its completion in the much more straightforward concept of a *recasting* of the experiential universe as a result of original sin. According to this second hypothesis, we could picture Adam and Eve, before the Fall, as forming a mankind more spiritual than our own. As a consequence of an infidelity similar to that of the angels, this pre-mankind would have become less spiritual, and more material; and it is in fact this materialization which would have produced the woeful multiplicity from which consciousness is

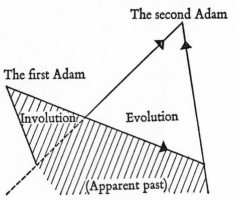

The second Adam

The first Adam

Involution

Evolution

(Apparent past)

now, in every quarter, painfully re-emerging. There are, thus, two phases to be considered in the complete cycle of the universe:

1. A phase of *involution* in matter (downward, centrifugal, fragmentation, starting from the first Adam), which resulted in the formation of the present earth;

2. A phase of *evolution towards* spirit (centripetal concentration, in the second Adam), whose goal is the bringing into being of the new earth. Scientifically, we can distinguish only the receding perspective of the second phase (since scientific analysis can only reconstruct the *evolutive* past); and we can even extend

that picture indefinitely, by applying our analysis, towards a progressively more dissociated multiplicity. However, not one of the series so disclosed will ever include Adam or Eve (since Adam and Eve belong to another picture).

This explanation of the 'recasting' of the world by the Fall fits in particularly well with a metaphysic of the 'idealist' type (by which I mean a metaphysic in which non-spiritual beings receive the fullness of their ontological actualizing from spiritual beings). But it is not an essential part of such a philosophy.

c. These two ways of conceiving original sin, explanation by 'switch or by recasting', both have the advantage of retaining the notion of an individual sinful act – even that of a first, personal, Adam (even though the personality in question can be no more than analogous to our own if, in order to avoid the difficulties of monogenism, we admit that the fall of the first man must have pluralized him). Where these two methods of representation fall down is that they force us into fantasy (that, at least, is what they appear to do at first: on reflection, we can see that this limitless receding view of the past is simply a pendant to the equally limitless prospects opened up by the reconstitution of the universe *in Christo*).

As a way of avoiding this objection, and also of ruling out what would appear to be *'esse sine necessitate'*,[2] I am inclined to favour a third explanation. This is that original sin expresses, translates, personifies, in an instantaneous and localized act, the perennial and universal law of imperfection which operates in mankind *in virtue* of its being '*in fieri*'.[3] One might even, perhaps, go so far as to say that since the creative act (by definition) causes being to rise up to God from the confines of nothingness (that is, from the depth of the multiple, which means from some other matter), all creation brings with it, as its accom-

2. 'Non-necessary being.'   3. 'In process of becoming.'

panying risk and shadow, some fault; in other words, it has its counterpart in some redemption. Seen in this way, the drama of Eden would be the very drama of the whole of human history concentrated in a symbol profoundly expressive of reality. Adam and Eve are images of mankind pressing on towards God. The beatitude of the earthly paradise is the salvation constantly offered to all, but rejected by many, and so arranged that nobody can succeed in obtaining it except by unification of his being in our Lord. (And what determines the *supernatural* character of this unification is that it is effected gratuitously around the Word and not around an infra-divine centre.)

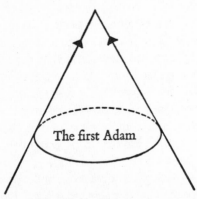

The first Adam

This way of understanding original sin, it is evident, gets rid of every difficulty that belongs to the scientific order: the transgression is inseparably merged in the evolution of the world. On the other hand, it has this disadvantage:

a. that we have to abandon an individual Adam and an initial fall, unless we regard as 'principal transgression' the moral crisis which apparently accompanied the first appearance of intelligence in man;

b. that, in consequence, it confuses in duration the two phases of fall and recovery; these are no longer two distinct periods, but two components which are constantly united in each man and in mankind.

Nevertheless, it may well be that what we regard as a disadvantage is in fact no more than the difficulty we have in abandoning our old, easier, ways of presenting it to our imagination. One thing is quite certain, that the traditional attitude towards God of spiritually minded Christians is retained whole and entire in views that appear to be so novel. In these views, I believe, it reaches the fullness of its intellectual and mystical development. Creation, Fall, Incarnation, Redemption, those vast universal events no longer appear as fleeting accidents occurring sporadically in time – a grossly immature view which is a perpetual offence to our reason and a contradiction of our experience. All four of those events become co-extensive with the duration and totality of the world; they are, in some way, aspects (distinct in reality but physically linked) of one and the same divine operation. The incarnation of the Word (which is in process of continual and universal consummation) is simply the final term of a creation which is still continuing everywhere and does so through our imperfections ('*omnis creatura adhuc ingemiscit et parturit*'[4] . . .). The supreme transgression, committed by an as yet inarticulate mankind, is not to be found behind us: would it not be better to look for it ahead, when mankind has at last become fully conscious of its powers and will split into two camps, for God or against him?[5]

4. 'The whole creation has been groaning in travail together until now' (Romans 8:22).

5. Père Teilhard's point of view, it should be noted, has much in common with what St Paul says about the eschatological increase of evil and the revelation of the 'man of lawlessness' at the coming of Christ (2 Thess. 2:3-11). That passage justifies our saying, as Teilhard very rightly pointed out, that the great sin of the world lies in the future, and that it will be a sin of apostasy.

Here, however, we enter the realm of dream. A more objective consideration in support of all solutions, no matter what form they take, which seek to explain the 'invisibility' of the Fall not by its smallness but by its inordinate magnitude, is as follows:

If we are to retain the Christian view of Christ-the-Redeemer, it is evident that we must also retain an original sin as vast as the world: otherwise Christ would have saved only a part of the world and would not be truly the centre of all. Further, scientific research has shown that, in space and duration, the world is vast beyond anything conceived by the apostles and the first generations of Christianity.

How, then, can we contrive still to make first original sin, and then the figure of Christ, cover the enormous and daily expanding panorama of the universe? How are we to maintain the possibility of *a fault as cosmic* as the Redemption?

The only way in which we can do so is by spreading the Fall throughout the whole of universal history, or at least by locating it *before a complete refashioning*, a recasting, of which the present order of things, in its experiential totality, would be the result.

We must so broaden our views on original sin that not only may scientists work with an easy mind, but Christians may be justified in fully loving a Christ whom they are forced to accept by no less than the whole urgent impact and plenitude of the universe; we must so expand our ideas that we shall find it impossible to locate original sin at any one point in our whole environment, and will realize simply that it is everywhere, as closely woven into the being of the world as the God who creates us and the Incarnate Word who redeems us.

N.B. Together with these attempts at an explanation, I may quote one (slightly amended) by Father Schmidt, which consists in saying: The earthly paradise never existed, since it represents above all a promise. Had man been faithful, the universe would have been guided towards a new state. This is the 'switch' solution, with the fork ahead missed. Among other disadvantages, this solution has that of leaving the difficulty of monogenism intact.

Unpublished, no date. Before Easter 1922.[6]

6. It was doubtless because of this note, intended for a study confined to theologians, but sent to the Superior General of the Jesuits in Rome, that Père Teilhard was obliged to give up teaching science at the Institut Catholique and take up geological work in China. Written early in the century, this essay was necessarily hesitant. Teilhard returned to its theme in 1947. Cf. p. 187.

PANTHEISM
AND CHRISTIANITY

IN this note I want to try to bring face to face two great religious powers: the only two powers, truth to say, that today share between them the world of human thought. They are Christianity and pantheism.

Generally speaking (when it is a Christian who is responsible for the confrontation) the chief concern is to emphasize the opposition between the two doctrines and to widen still further the gulf that divides them.

My approach in this essay will be the exact reverse. What I am proposing to do is to narrow that gap between pantheism and Christianity by bringing out what one might call the Christian soul of pantheism or the pantheist aspect of Christianity. My personal conviction is that it is with pantheism as it is with all the other isms (evolutionism, socialism, feminism, internationalism, modernism . . .). The designation of these words is, quite unwarrantably, restricted to certain particular, infelicitous and unacceptable, expressions of tendencies which, taken in their whole content, are legitimate; some day, there can be no doubt, they must be put in terms whose truth will be universally recognized. Pantheism has become synonymous with Spinozism, Hegelianism, theosophy, monism . . . I believe that this identification is false, unjustified and dangerous. Beneath the heterodox forms of the pantheist impulse just mentioned, there lie a psychological reality and an intellectual need which are much vaster and more enduring than any system of Hindu, Greek or German thought.

To put it briefly, my precise aim is as follows: I would like to make it clear that pantheism (in the current, restricted meaning of the word) is only the defective form in which is expressed a well-justified (and, moreover, ineradicable) tendency in the human soul, a tendency which can be fully satisfied only in Christianity.

This tendency is to recognize the *importance, in one's religious calculations, of the Whole.* In Part One I shall give a summary of its historical development, before considering, in Part Two, in what way it may be Christianized.

I. HISTORICAL DEVELOPMENT OF THE PANTHEIST TENDENCY

a. This feeling of the importance of the Whole has its roots in the furthest and most secret depths of our being. As a matter of intellectual necessity – as an affective need – and, maybe, by the direct impact made on us by the universe, we are constantly and essentially brought back to a consideration of the world, apprehended in its totality.

Initially, our intelligence is baffled by the multiple, by the plural. We are unable, in reality, to understand the multiple. We can comprehend beings only in so far as they can so escape from plurality as to be capable of action or reaction, of harmonization or association. For thought, the multiple (matter) is something without legitimate existence. The intelligible world, the true world, can only be a unified world. In consequence, the elements, the parts, the atoms, the monads, have no real and permanent value. Ultimately, the only thing that has any importance is the Whole, in which alone unity can be effected.

Parallel with (and in a sense identical with) our intellectual need of unity, we experience, deep within us, an affective and spontaneous need for union. Man is not drawn towards the One (that is, the Whole) by his reason alone, but by the full force of his whole being (is not our thought the act of our whole being?). On earth we are essentially separate, incomplete

– a point made, you may remember, in Plato's *Phaedrus*. We are seeking desperately for our completion; and we cannot find it by wedding ourselves to any element of the world taken in isolation. What we reach out to grasp in our aspirations is something which is diffused throughout, which permeates, everything. Fundamentally, we have but one passion: to become one with the world which envelops us without our ever being able to distinguish either its face or its heart. Would man worship woman if he did not believe that he saw the universe mirrored in her eyes? And does man continue to love woman when (by his own fault) he has reduced her to no more than one poor closed individual, opening the road for him to no further extension either of his race or of his ideal?

Ultimately, our thought cannot comprehend anything but the Whole, nor, when it really comes to the point, can our dreams entertain anything but the Whole. Should we go further and say that there are times when the Whole makes itself directly manifest to us – when it almost intuitively forces itself upon us? It may well be so. When we read the evidence of certain Christian or pagan mystics, or even simply what many perfectly ordinary people may tell us in confidence, we cannot but quite seriously question whether there may not be a sort of cosmic consciousness in our soul, more diffuse than our personal consciousness, more intermittent, but perfectly well-defined – a sort of feeling of the presence of all beings at the same time, so that they are not perceived as multiple and separate but as forming part of one and the same unit, at least in the future ... Whether this consciousness of the universal is a reality, or whether it is the materialization of a wish, of an expectation – that is a question for the psychologists to answer, if they can. The least one may say is that many people have believed that they have experienced 'cosmic consciousness', so that, even if it is not an independent source through which we are introduced to a consideration of the Whole, at least it shows

– since we tend to objectivize our dream – how immensely strong is our feeling of the importance of the Whole.

b. If it is true that our concern for the Whole is as deeply rooted in the human as I have just maintained, we should not be surprised to find the pantheist current (in the wide sense of the word) incorporated in the first historical manifestations of human thought.

In its vaguest, but most innate and persistent form, we see the feeling of the Whole as the fertilizer of poetic genius. Whether their theme be the great cosmogonic myths, great wars, great passions, or the grandeurs of nature, poets have never been truly poets (nor will they ever be) except in so far as they have responded to some flash of the absolute, of the universal making itself apparent to them in one or other of the manifestations, infra- or super-human, of the universal generative force: of Demeter. We may say, I believe, that there is no profound poetry, no true lyricism, no sublimity in words, in art or in music, that does not rest upon evocation of the Whole, presentiment of, nostalgia for, the Whole. And yet there have always been poets: there must, then, always have been naturally pantheist souls.

Philosophers, too, of all times have tried to record the exact characteristics of, and to systematize, what poets of all times have experienced and celebrated when this universal vibration reverberated in their souls – either because the philosophers also had this world-feeling, or simply because they wanted to understand what the poets meant. There is no need for me to labour the point – you can see it in the powerful ventures into monism of the earliest Greek philosophers, and in the Alexandrians' subtle attempts to establish the existence of the Logos, and in the Stoics' contemplation of the soul of the world.

This may be remarkable, but it is in no way surprising. Whether expressed in poetic impulse or in philosophical constructions, pantheism in the wide sense in which I am now discussing it, as referring, that is, to a concern for the Whole, is seen to be religious, fundamentally religious. From beneath the most secular experience of love (provided it be deep), from beneath the most coldly reasoned construction of the universe (provided it seek to embrace the whole of the real) there always shines through some divine emotion, and over it there passes a breath of worship. How, indeed, could it be otherwise? With its attributes of (at least relative) universality, unity, and infallibility, the Whole cannot reveal itself to us without our recognizing in it God, or the shadow of God. And on his side, how can God make himself manifest to us otherwise than by passing through the Whole, by assuming the features or at least the outward integument of the Whole?

Poet, philosopher, mystic – it is hardly possible to be one without being the others. In the great stream of past mankind, poets, philosophers, and mystics – the long procession of those who have been initiated into the vision and cult of the Whole – have left behind them a central wake which we can follow unmistakably from our own days right back to the most distant horizons of history. In one sense, therefore, we may say that a concern for the Whole is extremely ancient. It belongs to all ages. From another angle, however (and this is a point that must be fully understood), it seems in our day to be going through a real crisis of awakening. It is highly peculiar to our own time. As I shall briefly demonstrate, we may say, in fact, that the essentially modern work of philosophic criticism and scientific research which has been carried out for the last two or three centuries in every field of terrestrial knowledge, is all leading in the same direction: by an astonishing convergence of all its findings, we can see that it is directly contributing to a magnification and solidification of the universe as one bloc.

In philosophy, in the first place, rigorously pursued analysis of the conditions of knowledge has brought out with increased force what medieval thought, both Arab and Christian, had already seen – that each centre of consciousness in the world could not know the world as it is in fact capable of knowing it, except by being co-extensive with it. If the consciousness of each monad is to be explicable, that monad must be conceived not as an atom juxtaposed with other atoms, but as a partial centre of the Whole, a particular outlook on the Whole, a particular actualizing of the Whole.[1] We must, however, go still further in the ontological consolidation of the universe. The most extraordinary thing about the phenomenon of knowledge is not that each one of us can understand the world. The really amazing thing is that the countless points of view represented by our individual thoughts should have a point of coincidence; that, intellectually, we should all appreciate one and the same pattern in the universe; that we should understand one another. The reason for the existence of this mutual understanding, of this intellectual concurrence in our collective penetration of the real, can be found only in the existence of a principle which controls and unifies individual perceptions. If, therefore, we are to explain the effective operation of human thought, something more is needed than the fact that each consciousness is co-extensive with the whole of the knowable. We must go further and admit that all consciousnesses, taken as one whole, are dominated, influenced and guided by a sort of higher consciousness; and that it is this which animates, governs and synthesizes all the different apprehensions of the universe effected by each monad in isolation. Not only is each one of us partially Whole – we are all together included in, given cohesion in, a unifying association. There is a centre which is the centre of all the centres, and without which the entire edifice of thought would disintegrate into dust.

In recent times physics (by which I mean all the natural

1. Here Teilhard is expressing concretely in terms of the 'Whole' what traditional philosophy expresses abstractly in terms of 'Being'.

sciences) has gradually made its way, by humbler and more roundabout roads than metaphysics, towards equally grand horizons. All the progress we have made, since the Renaissance, in penetrating nature derives, indeed, from what may be expressed in just these few words: The discovery of the universe's infinite extension and infinite cohesion in space and time.

First, in space, we have witnessed the gradual and astonishing emergence and analysis of the twofold infinity of vastness and minuteness. At the present moment (pending, that is, further discoveries) we stand between two extreme terms of material elements, the electron and the nebula. And within this wide spectrum of corpuscular magnitudes, to whose lines there would appear to be no limit either in length or number, there prevails an unimaginable solidarity; operating through the mysterious zones of the ether and of gravity, this knits everything that exists into an extraordinary continuum of energy. The greater the world grows as we explore it, the more advanced the interpenetration of its elements. In the order of measurable energy, everything holds together; and the same is equally true in the more fugitive, more complex, but no less physically real domain of the soul's organic developments and experiential manifestations. In truth, the world, as seen by science, stretches out immeasurably and at the same time forms one solid block in space.

In time, we find the same phenomenon of growth and fusion – but with an even more shattering impact! Without any doubt, the great advance made by human thought in modern times has been its reaching an awareness of time, of the perspectives opened up by time, of the way beings form a chain-series in time. Not so very long ago one could be confronted by a mountain, a living creature, a spoken language, a social type, a form of religion, without bothering about where they came from, or at any rate without doubting but that they had always existed just as we see them now. Today we have learnt to adjust our vision in a completely different way. No longer do we see every reality in the world as a product interpolated instantaneously, at a given time T, into all the other realities of the world; the beginning of everything is hidden from us. No object is scientifically intelligible to us except as the culmination of a limitless series of prior states. History is invading and tending to absorb the whole of science. After first making its way into living things, which are more open to its attacks, we now find it doing the same to inorganic bodies. We now realize that there is not an atom which, if it were to be fully understood, would not have to be followed ever further and further into its past, through the endless series of its earlier states. Not only does the whole of the present world reverberate in every fragment of the world, but, in some way, the whole of the past world reaches its term in it.

Thus, from the patient, prosaic, but cumulative work of scientists of all types, there has spontaneously emerged the most impressive revelation of the Whole that could possibly be conceived. What the ancient poets, philosophers and mystics had glimpsed or discovered (primarily by intuition), what modern philosophy demands, more rigorously, in the order of metaphysics, science of today has brought within our grasp even in its lower, sensibly apprehensible, zones. Today the universe, in its totality and unity, forces itself inexorably on our attention. Whatever the avenue opened up by our thought and our activity, there it stands, whole and entire, to be a burden to us, to fascinate us, or to exalt us.

In the moral sphere the effects of a like 'epiphany' cannot but be enormous. However positivist the intentions with which we embark on a study of the Whole, the mode of its reaction on those who contemplate it is, as I was saying, inevitably religious. And we find the same inevitable consequence, again, following the more direct and more magnificent revelation of the universe which belongs peculiarly to our own century: it has operated on the mystical tendencies to unity and union which are common to mankind of all ages, and has thereby directed a great surge of worship towards the world.

Explicit or in a disguised form, we can see the worship of the world in every quarter, wherever we look. It would be no exaggeration to say that it dominates modern religious history. It is that worship which seeks for expression in the present proliferation of neo-Buddhisms, of theosophies, of spiritualistic doctrines. It is that, basically, which in an ill-defined way is driving the masses towards some sort of progress, some sort of super-mankind. Were one able to make one's way to the bottom of men's souls, one would find that worship sustaining the most unbelieving of scientists in his researches. On almost every occasion it is that which provides a refuge for the best minds that abandon the various Christian forms of belief. And finally, as we can recognize by countless symptoms, it is that worship which is seeking to make its way into the formulation of the most orthodox faith.

Nobody, I think, can fail to see that the vital question for Christianity today is to decide what attitude believers will adopt towards this recognition of the value of the Whole, this 'preoccupation with the Whole'. Will they open their hearts to it, or will they reject it as an evil spirit?

It is obviously a very difficult question to answer. In the first place, for many historical and psychological reasons, the religion of the Whole has hitherto been expressed primarily in terms of paganism and anti-Christianity. Whether because the Christian God seemed useless and distant, or even maleficent, in comparison with the powerful evolution immanent in things – or whether because philosophic thought believed that it found its perfect expression in a monism which united beings to a degree at which all distinction was lost – the fact remains that the great mass of those who follow the religion of the Whole have abandoned Christianity. And now it might well appear that all is over for ever between them and us, the followers of Jesus Christ: '*Chaos firmatum est*', the reign of Chaos is established.

There can be no immediate truce, therefore, with such opponents. On the other hand, however, how can we condemn and repudiate them unreservedly, '*simpliciter*', without severe damage to ourselves? If we have nothing but reproach for them and banish them indiscriminately from our communion, the pantheists will certainly take with them the most vital part of this world which it is our professed aim to save and lead back to God. Passion for the Whole, we must remember, is neither a free decision nor an artificial product; it represents the most active part (maybe, indeed, all) of this natural mysticism of which Christian mysticism can only be the sublimation and crowning peak. Moreover, science and philosophy's revelation of the Whole is an undeniable fact. For the believer, as for every man who can see and think, the universe stands out with an organic unity, a coherence, a compelling emphasis, a brilliance, that dazzle us, no matter how tightly we screw up our eyes. How could the Christian live, cut off from the vital source which feeds mankind's fundamental religious feeling? How could he calmly worship his Father in heaven, so long as he was surrounded, as though by an ubiquitous temptation, by the influence, the shadow, of the universal and moving reality of the cosmos?

Truth to say, there is only one attitude Christianity may adopt towards the persistent, and to some degree legitimate, rise of the religion of the Whole: it must directly confront the spellbinding grandeur that is revealing itself – overcome it, take possession of it, and assimilate it. The present religious crisis derives from the antagonism between the God of supernatural revelation on one side and the great mysterious figure of the universe on the other; in consequence there will be no permanent peace for our faith unless we succeed in understanding that God and the cosmos are not real enemies – that there is no opposition between them – but that what *is* possible is a conjunction between the two stars whose pull in opposite directions may well tear apart our souls. If we are to convert the earth and give it peace, today, we must see and make our fellow-men see that it is God himself who is pulling them and making his influence felt on them through the unifying process of the universe.

Is such an enterprise possible? Of course it is; but on one condition, that we understand with all the necessary realism the mystery of the Incarnation.

II. CHRISTIAN TRANSPOSITION OF
THE FUNDAMENTAL PANTHEIST TENDENCY

Nothing in our progressive world is truly intelligible until it has reached its end. It is only at the end of our lives, when you come to think of it, that each one of us understands himself with anything like correctness. If, then, we are to obtain a true idea of the Incarnation we must not go back to its beginnings (the Annunciation, the Nativity, even the Passion); our standpoint, so far as possible, must be its final term. We cannot, of course, anticipate the vast expanse of duration which still separates us from the establishment of the kingdom of God; for a long time still, the consummation of that kingdom outruns any distinct imaginative effort. At the same time, however, we have Scripture (St Paul, in particular) to tell us what, in a general way, will be the final appearance of the world restored in Jesus Christ. Let us, then, see whether, in examining the features of this new earth, we may not find a way of arriving at a new interpretation that will fit in with both the expectations of the pantheist and the hopes of the Christian.

St Paul gives us to understand that the happiness of the elect should not be understood as a solitary, self-centred enjoyment of God. On the contrary, heaven will consist in the close association of all the elect, gathered into one single body under the influence of their head, Jesus Christ. However individual our salvation may be from many points of view, it is in consequence accomplished only in a collective fulfilment. The heavenly Jerusalem, the Apocalypse tells us, knows but one medium of knowledge and action: the illuminating and unifying radiance emanating from the God-man. 'In those days there will be no need of sun to shine, for its light is the Lamb.'[2] We shall be saved, and we shall see God only in so far as we are one in Christ Jesus. The Incarnation ends in the building up of a living church, of a mystical body, of a consummated totality, of a pleroma (to use St Paul's word that defies translation); that is a fact – a dogma – which all believers concur in accepting. Up to that point there is universal agreement about the nature of the Incarnation.

Where we find a serious divergence of opinion (whether instinctive or rational) among theologians and the faithful is when it comes to specifying what sort of bonds hold together the members of Christ's mystical body, the elements of the pleroma. How are we to understand the consistence of this mysterious organism? By analogy with the strong physical associations we see effected in our own environment, in the domain of natural beings? Or should we understand it by analogy only with the moral, artificial groupings which it is a daily occurrence for us to form or dissolve in the juridical domain of social relationships? Depending on how they answer this question – on which side of the fence they come down – orthodox Christians are divided into two categories; and the irreconcilable opposition between the two is curiously apparent in a wide range of different fields (dogmatic, moral, and mystical), but nowhere more forcibly than in the question

2. After Rev. 21:23: 'And the city has no need of sun or moon to shine upon it, for the glory of God is its light, and its lamp is the Lamb.'

with which we are now concerned – in that of the relationship between Christianity and the pantheist tendencies of the human soul.

There can be no hiding the fact: in the present teaching of theology and ascetics, the most prominent tendency is to give the word 'mystical' (in mystical body, mystical union) a minimum of organic or physical meaning. It may be due to the influence of the language of the Gospels, which are so inclined to announce and describe the kingdom of God in terms of the family or of society; or it may be because to build up a theology it is much simpler and safer to deal with juridical relationships and moral attachments (whose content and limits can be defined as closely as one wishes) than with physical relationships and organic connexions (which to a large extent refuse to be contained in our intellectual constructions); but, whatever the reason, the official Church normally shrinks from emphasizing the concrete, realistic, character of the terms in which the Scripture defines the state of unification attained by the consummated universe. Many experts in the theory of Catholicism, it is true, maintain against the Protestants that sanctifying grace, the life-blood which pours out from Christ to vivify the Church, is not a mere qualification or characteristic, external to the soul, but an undoubted physical reality, a new and higher life, which super-animates our rational life. At the same time, even so, they speak of heaven as though the bond established by justification between Christ and the Christian were of a sort of infra-physical nature. Without realizing it, they make the very common mistake of regarding the spiritual as an attenuation of the material, whereas it is in fact the material carried beyond itself: it is super-material. Thus what they make of the mystical body – of the pleroma – is primarily a vast association, a family on a very large scale, in which the individuals are held together principally by bonds of common agreement and affection. If Christian hopes could find true expression only in words of this order (which, it must be admitted, are pretty colourless) then we should have to give up any idea of Christianizing the recognition of the importance of the Whole, the religion of the Whole. For the Christians whose intellectual position we have just outlined, all that exists, in fact, on earth as in heaven, is an aggregation, based on agreement, of parts which are arbitrarily creatable and interchangeable; neither in the present universe, nor in the restored world, can any Whole be said truly to exist.

Fortunately, the man who is true to Christ's teaching can entertain more powerful (and more modern) views; and he has good grounds for attributing to the supernatural organism to which he believes himself to be linked a structure at least as consistent as that which we see in the tangible realities of the natural cosmos. Without any doubt, we Christians can (and, indeed, what is much more, we must) understand the mystical union of the elect in Christ as combining the warm flexibility of social relationships with the imperative rigour and irreversibility of the physical and biological laws or attractive forces operating in the present universe. That is just the point which I wished to lead up to in this lecture.

When we try to understand and express in physical terms the way in which the mystical body (the pleroma) is held together, there is, of course, one extreme we must avoid if we are not to 'founder in our faith'. We should not do what could be read into the language censured in some mystics (Eckhart, for example) and try to make of the consummated Christ a being so unique that his subsistence, his person, his 'I', takes the place of the subsistence, the personality, of all the elements incorporated in his mystical body. This concept of a hypostatic union extended to the whole universe (which, incidentally, is simply Spinoza's pantheism) is not in itself either contradictory or absurd; but it conflicts with the whole Christian view of individual freedom and personal salvation. There is, however, no difficulty in avoiding the exaggerated 'physicism' introduced by this attempt to express the unification of the world in Jesus Christ. Without having to fall back on monism, there are, in fact, plenty of ways of conceiving a 'graduated' type of union for the pleroma (modified by the very excess of its physical perfection), such that, without losing anything of their subsistence or personality, the elect would be *physically* incorporated in the organic and 'natural' whole of the consummated Christ. Take, for example, the stones in a vault or the cells in a living body such as our own. Each stone has its own particular shape, and each cell has its own activity, and often its own movement; and yet without the vault no stone can be completely understood in its shape or maintain its equilibrium in space; nor can any cell be explained or live in the full sense of the word outside the complete body. Each stone is itself plus the vault – each cell is itself plus ourselves. These comparisons are faulty because of the imperfection of the control exercised, mechanically by the whole of the vault and biologically by the human soul – the result of that imperfection being that the individuality of the elements of stone or protoplasm is hardly allowed to emerge or is partially suppressed by the dominating 'form'. But imagine a unifying influence so powerful and so perfect that the further its assimilation of the elements was carried (a function which would seem to be eminently characteristic of true unification), the more it would accentuate their differentiation. Thinking along those lines we can arrive at an idea of the mystical body of Christ which indeed appears both to satisfy the legitimate 'pantheist' aspirations of our minds and hearts, and to allow Christian dogma and mysticism the only environment in which they can develop freely.

In the first place, if in his interpretation of the process of the Incarnation a Christian adopts the eminently justifiable point of view which rests on organic and physical analogies, then nothing in the world any longer subsists permanently for him apart from the unifying influence of Christ. Throughout the whole range of things Christ is the principle of universal consistence: '*In eo omnia constant.*'[3] For such a Christian, exactly as for the modern philosopher, the universe has no complete reality except in the movement which causes all its elements to converge upon a number of higher centres of cohesion (in other words, which spiritualizes them); nothing holds together absolutely except through the Whole; and the Whole itself holds together only through its future fulfilment. On the other hand, unlike the free-thinking philosopher, the Christian can say that he already stands in a personal relationship with the centre of the world; for him, in fact, that centre is Christ – it is Christ who in a real and unmetaphorical sense of the word holds up the universe. So incredible a cosmic function may well be too much for our imagination, but I do not see how we could possibly avoid attributing it to the Son of Mary. The Incarnate Word could not be the supernatural (hyper-physical) centre of the universe if he did not function *first* as its physical, natural, centre. Christ cannot sublimate creation in God without progressively raising it up by his influence through the successive circles of matter and spirit. That is why, in order to bring all things back to his Father, he had to make himself one with all – he had to enter into contact with every one of the zones of the created, from the lowest and most earthly to the zone that is closest to heaven. '*Quid est quod ascendit in coelum, nisi prius quod descendit in ima terrae ut repleret omnia.*'[4] Even, therefore, in that aspect of its evolution which

3. 'In him all things hold together' (Col. 1:17).

4. 'What is he who rose up to heaven but that which first came down to the lowest depths of earth that it might fill all things?' – a quotation based on St Paul's words in Ephesians 4:9-10: '*Quod autem ascendit, quid est, nisi quia et descendit primum in inferiores partes terrae? Qui descendit, ipse est et qui ascendit super omnes coelos, ut impleret omnia.*' 'In saying, "He ascended", what does it mean but that he also descended into the lower parts of the

is regarded as the most 'natural', it is towards Christ that the universe, since all time, has been moving as one integral whole. '*Omnis creatura usque adhuc ingemiscit et parturit.*'[5] Has any evolutionist pantheism, in fact, ever spoken more magnificently of the Whole than St Paul did in the words he addressed to the first Christians? This might, perhaps, seem a dangerous view – as though such a boundless prospect might prove so absorbing as to make the man who entertains it forget his humble practical duties and the solid virtues of the Gospels. Its effect is, in fact, the exact opposite: when one understands how physical and immediate is the omni-influence of Christ, the vigour assumed by every detail of the Christian life is quite astonishing; it gains an emphasis never dreamt of by those who are frightened of the realistic view of the mystery of the Incarnation.

Take charity, for example, that complete change of attitude so insistently taught by Christ. It has nothing in common with our colourless philanthropy, but represents the essential affinity which brings men closer together, not in the superficial sphere of sensible affections or earthly interests, but in building up the pleroma.

The possibility, and even the obligation of doing everything for God ('*Quidquid facitis, in nomine Domini nostri Jesu Christi facite*')[6] are no longer based solely on the virtue of obedience, or solely on the moral value of intention; they can be explained, in short, only by the marvellous grace, instilled into every human effort, no matter how material, of effectively co-

---

earth? He who descended is he also who ascended far above all the heavens, that he might fill all things.'

5. After Romans 8:22: 'The whole creation has been groaning in travail together until now.'

6. 'Whatever you do . . . do everything in the name of the Lord Jesus' (Col. 3:17).

operating, through its physical result, in the fulfilment of the body of Christ.

Salvation and damnation, again, are no longer simply the blessing or curse that falls arbitrarily on the being, from outside. Those two words now mean something much more formidable. They affect the whole relationship of the element to the centre of universal cohesion, that is of universal beatification: either incorporation in it, which brings fulfilment, or severance from it, which brings loss of organic structure.

It is the same with imitation of Christ; this is something quite different from the Christian's conforming outwardly to a humble, arduous life of simple faith. To 'conform' to Christ is to share through a partial identity, in the unique, fundamental act constituted by the Whole. There is, in reality, *only one* humility in the world, *one* loving-kindness, *one* sacrifice, *one* passion, *one* laying in the tomb, *one* resurrection – and it is Christ's. It is all one in him, multiple in us – begun and perfected by him, and yet completed by us.

The greatest change, however, comes with mass and communion, when we realize the full depth and universality of their mystery. We now understand that when Christ descends sacramentally into each one of his faithful it is not simply in order to commune with him; it is in order to join him, physically, a little more closely to himself and to all the rest of the faithful in the growing unity of the world. When, through the priest, Christ says, '*Hoc est corpus meum*', 'This is my body', the words reach out infinitely far beyond the morsel of bread over which they are pronounced: they bring the entire mystical body into being. The priestly act extends beyond the transubstantiated Host to the cosmos itself, which, century after century, is gradually being transformed by the Incarnation, itself never complete. From age to age, there is but one single mass in the world: the true Host, the total Host, is the universe which is continually being more intimately penetrated and vivified by Christ. From the most distant origin of things until their unforeseeable consummation, through the countless convulsions of boundless space, the whole of nature is slowly and irresistibly undergoing the supreme consecration. Fundamentally – since all time and for ever – but one single thing is being made in creation: the body of Christ.

If I wished fully to express the mysteries and the practical application of our faith, translating them into terms of organic and physical realities, I should have endlessly to multiply such considerations. And yet, I believe, the phrase I have used says everything that is needed: 'One single thing is being made.'

'One single thing is being made.' Whose is the phrase – the Christian's? Or the pantheist's?

The Christian's, without a shadow of doubt, since the believer who uses it as I have just done knows that in the powerful embrace of the omnipresent Christ, souls do not lose their personality, but win it. It is, indeed, a Christian who has thus stolen the pantheist's fire, the fire with which he threatened to set the earth ablaze with an incandescence that would not have been Christ's.

The Christian who has understood the universal function exercised by the incarnate God is more successful in his 'unitarian' attempt than the pantheist. The latter, while claiming to unify beings, merges them in an undifferentiated whole; which means, in fact, that his monism annihilates the mystery and joy of union. The Christian, on the other hand, has really arrived at the central and impregnable position from which, looking down from the security of his possession of the world, he can radiate his faith and his hope.

There is now solid confirmation for his hope. When it is borne in upon his consciousness that the dimensions of the universe are still increasing immeasurably (as they have been for the last three centuries) he will no longer fear that the countenance and brilliance of the revealed God he worships may be eclipsed by the new star. How could either of these two majestic grandeurs dim the radiance of the other? The one is but the peak – the soul, we might say – of the other. Christ is clothed in the earth: let this earth, then, grow ever greater, that Christ's raiment may be ever more magnificent! Christ guides from within the universal progress of the world: may our consciousness, then, of the bond that runs through all things, of their constant movement in being, grow ever more keen, and so make the impact of Christ upon us ever greater.

Already, at this very moment, by everything we do, we all share in all, through and in him whom we might think distant from us, but in whom, quite literally, '*vivimus, movemur et sumus*'.[7] A little while yet – what hope could be grander? – creation, totally dominated by Christ, will be lost in him and through him within the final and permanent unity, where (in St Paul's very words, the most clear-cut assertion we have of Christian 'pantheism') '*ἔσται ὁ Θεὸς πάντα ἐν πᾶσιν*'.[8]

Unpublished lecture, Paris, 1923.

7. We live and move and have our being' (Acts 17:28).
8. 'God will be all in all', after 1 Cor. 15:28.

CHRISTOLOGY AND EVOLUTION

I can see Christ only as I depict him here. But what matters to me is not so much the colours in which I portray him as his integrity. It is in this spirit that I write what follows – in the hope of serving Christ.

THE PROBLEM

THERE is nothing completely new in the substance of this essay; still less can I say that the form is final and definitive. It is simply an attempt to express views that I have already put forward on a number of occasions (in particular in *Le Milieu Divin* (*The Divine Milieu*) and *Le Sens de la Terre*) – and to focus them more sharply, and in terms that, while more hard and fast, will also be easier to rectify.

To my mind, the whole internal vitality (and in consequence the whole diffusive power) of Christianity depends today on finding a solution to a problem that has always been shelved. What that problem is I shall try to explain as clearly as I can by asking this question: 'What form must our Christology take if it is to remain itself in a new world?'

The presupposition underlying this problem, and accepted by all Christians, is that our religion is essentially perception of the universe and coming to practical terms with it '*in Christo Jesu*'. We can explain the universe and live in it only '*per Ipsum*' and '*in Ipso*' (through him and in him): the drive and joy specific in the act of Christian worship are concentrated in that single dogmatic point.

However, like every other living reality, that force and that joyfulness have their arduous counterpart. As we are beginning to learn by experience, the universe is not a fixed framework upon which we have simply to project the image of Christ so that we can then quietly admire it for the rest of our days. Precisely under the influence of what we call life, the screen of the world (unlike the symbolic wild ass's skin)[1] expands and wraps itself in folds around us. Unless we are very careful we shall find that the divine countenance, which should embrace all things, is projected on them only as a blurred outline, or covers but a part of them.

My profound conviction, born of the experience of a life spent simultaneously in the heart of the Gentile world and in that of the Church, is that at this very moment we have reached a delicate point of balance at which a readjustment is essential. It could not, in fact, be otherwise: our Christology is still expressed in exactly the same terms as those which, three centuries ago, could satisfy men whose outlook on the cosmos it is now physically impossible for us to accept. Unless we admit that religious life and human life are independent of one another (which is a psychological impossibility) such a situation must *a priori* produce a feeling of dismay, a loss of balance. That it has already done so cannot be denied. I can testify to this in my own case, and the whole of what we call the modernist movement bears me out. What we now have to do without delay is to modify the position occupied by the central core of Christianity – and this precisely in order that it may not lose its illuminative value.

If we ask in what exactly this correction in *relationship* consists, the answer must be in bringing Christology and evolution into line with one another.

The quite recent (and still continuing) transformation which has taken the universe from a state of static reality to one of evolutive reality, has all the characteristics of a deep-rooted and definitive event. All that could be said in criticism of it is that

1. In Balzac's *La Peau de Chagrin*.

we are still a long way from completely appreciating the extent of the changes logically entailed by perception of this new cosmic dimension: Duration. The universe is no longer endless in space alone. In all its strands, it now unfolds interminably into the past, governed by a constantly active cosmogenesis. It would be superfluous to analyse the breadth or the forward drive – both irresistible – of this new outlook, which is basically characteristic of what we call 'the modern spirit'. I need do no more than note that at the present moment human knowledge is developing exclusively under the aegis of evolution, recognized as a prime property of experiential reality. So true is this that *nothing can any longer find place in our constructions which does not first satisfy the conditions* of a universe in process of transformation. A Christ whose features do not adapt themselves to the requirements of a world that is evolutive in structure will tend more and more to be eliminated out of hand – just as in learned societies today articles on perpetual motion or squaring the circle are consigned to the wastepaper-basket, unread. And correspondingly, if a Christ is to be completely acceptable as an object of worship, he must be presented as the saviour of the idea and reality of evolution.

This is where we may profitably make an experiment, but we must do so logically, carrying it through to the end, if only to see what the result will be. Take the world, honestly, as we see it today in the light of reason; not the four-thousand-year-old world, surrounded by its eight or nine spheres *for which the theology of our textbooks was written*, but the universe which we can see organically emerging from a boundless time and space. Spread out this vast, infinitely receding panorama, and then let us try to see how we shall have to modify Christ's apparent contours if his figure is to continue today, *just as before*, to stamp itself triumphantly on everything. It is this new Christ (and not the obsolete figure which perhaps we might prefer factitiously to preserve) which will in reality be the former, the true Jesus. We shall recognize him by this sign of a universal presence.

It is along three axes, we might say, that we are going to attempt this complete covering of the world by Christ. Redemption, Incarnation, the gospel message: how are these three aspects of Christology to be modified if they are to measure up to the properties of an evolutive world?

I. REDEMPTION

Whenever we try intellectually and vitally to assimilate Christianity with all our modern soul, the first obstacles we meet always derive from original sin.

This applies in the first place to scientific research, where the traditional representation of the Fall is a decisive barrier against any advance towards a broadened outlook on the world. The fact is that it is the determination to preserve the literal interpretation of the story of the Fall which accounts for the stubbornness with which the concrete reality of the first human couple is defended. Foreign though it is to the scale and shape of our present scientific views, the retention of this element is sufficient in itself to paralyse or vitiate every attempt made by a scientist who is also a believer to construct a satisfactory picture of universal history.

Strictly speaking, however, this difficulty still belongs only to the intellectual order. The real position is even more serious. From the point of view of the Christian scientist, acceptance of Adam and Eve necessarily means that history is cut off short in a completely unreal way at the level of the appearance of man; but what is more, when we reach the more immediately living domain of belief, original sin, in its present representation, is a constant bar to the natural development of our religion. It clips the wings of hope: we are incessantly eager to launch out into the wide open field of conquest which optimism suggests, and every time it drags us back inexorably into the *overpowering* darkness of reparation and expiation.

The more I study the matter, the more I am forced to accept this evidence that original sin, conceived in the form still attributed to it today, is an intellectual and emotional strait-jacket. What lies behind this pernicious quality it possesses, and to whom can we look for release?[2]

To my mind, the answer is that if the dogma of original sin is constricting and debilitating it is simply because, as now expressed, it represents a survival of obsolete static views into our now evolutionary way of thinking. Fundamentally, in fact, the idea of Fall is no more than an attempt to explain evil in a fixed universe. As such, it is completely out of keeping with the rest of our representations of the world; and that is why we find it oppressive. If, therefore, we are to have an atmosphere in which we can breathe, we must make a fresh approach to the problem of evil, in its relationship to Christ, and rethink it in terms that fit in with our new cosmic views.

Original sin is *a static solution of the problem of evil.*

In days gone by, this major premise brought me a flat denial from a theological censor; but even now I can still find no way of denying that it is true.

Logically, in the first place, disorder cannot be explained in a universe which is presumed to have issued *fully formed* from the hand of God except by a *secondary* distortion of the world. The corruptibility of organisms, the flesh and spirit duality, and the glaring disorders of society are a sheer intellectual stumbling-block for those whose static cosmos demands one

2. To see that this is no exaggeration, one has only to read Pius XI's encyclical on the Sacred Heart (for example, the sixth lesson in the Breviary for the Sunday within the octave of the feast of the Sacred Heart). There are sentences in it which are at least as severe a blow to the most legitimate hopes of the modern soul as was the Syllabus itself. That is not the spirit by which the world will ever be converted. (Note by Père Teilhard.)

single creation. In themselves, these effects should not exist; further, because they entail suffering they suggest the punishments which every human group decides to inflict on those who upset the established order. The quite natural confluence of these two factors has inevitably produced the idea that the world is doing penance for a fault committed in the past.

Factually speaking, is not that precisely the point of view of the Bible and the Epistle to the Romans?

'Through sin comes death.' In order to get away from evidence that is only too clear, an attempt is now being made to weaken this illuminating phrase. 'Death, it is agreed, most certainly existed for animals before man's transgression; and, had man been faithful, even in his case it could not have been averted except by a sort of permanent miracle.' However, not only do these distinctions still leave the problem of evil intact, they contradict the obvious meaning of the biblical text. For St Paul, we must remember, the world was only a week old when Adam sinned. Nothing in paradise, accordingly, had yet had time to perish. In the mind of the apostle, it was that transgression which ruined everything for the whole of creation.

In spite of the subtle distinctions of the theologians, it is a matter *of fact* that Christianity has developed under the overriding impression that all the evil around us was *born from an initial transgression*. So far as dogma is concerned, we are still living in the atmosphere of a universe in which what matters most is reparation and expiation. The vital problem, both for Christ and ourselves, is to get rid of a stain. This accounts for the importance, at least in theory, of the idea of sacrifice, and for the interpretation of baptism almost exclusively in terms of purification. It explains, too, the pre-eminence in Christology of the idea of redemption and the shedding of blood. It is, in short, because Christ is still today projected upon a static world, as he used to be, that he is presented to us in official ecclesiastical documents chiefly through *the shadow of his cross.*

Supposing, however, we now try, if only by some trick of the mind, to shift our outlook *unreservedly* into that of a world which is evolving?

A fundamental change, pregnant with consequences for Christology, immediately begins to become apparent in our views. In this new setting, while evil loses nothing of its poignancy or horror, it ceases to be an incomprehensible element in the structure of the world and becomes *a natural feature.*

At this point, I know, I am beginning to come into conflict with some of my dearest intellectual friends. For reasons derived from the omnipotence of God or from the metaphysical nature of the multiple, they will not accept what I am going to say. Nevertheless I am still convinced that there is a logic in things to which everything must bow, and that in a universe (or, more correctly, an ontology) that is evolutive in type this logic imposes on the creative act conditions such as *inevitably* to entail evil as a secondary effect. To create had hitherto been regarded as a divine operation capable of assuming completely arbitrary forms. We used to accept, at least implicitly, that God was free and had the power to raise up participated being in any state of perfection and association he chose. He could position it, as he pleased, at the level of any point whatsoever between zero and infinity. It seems to me impossible to reconcile these imaginary views with the most fundamental conditions of being, as manifest in our experience. There is only one way I can see of providing a steady foundation for our concepts of possible relationships between God and the world; and it is as follows.

To create, even when we use the word omnipotence,[3] must

---

3. It is one of the weaknesses of Christian philosophy that it misrepresents the omnipotence of God to the point of multiplying endlessly the contingent and the arbitrary in the universe. Yet there are many things which it is

no longer be understood as an instantaneous act but as a process or controlled movement of synthesis. Pure act and 'non-being' are diametrically opposed in the same way as are perfected unity and pure multiple. This means that in spite of (or rather because of) his perfections, the Creator cannot communicate himself immediately to his creature, but must make the creature capable of receiving him. If God is to be able to give himself to the plural, he must unify it to his own measure. In consequence, the constitution of the pleroma, from the origins of the world until God, must necessarily make itself apparent to our minds by a progressive advance of spirit.

We must, however, go further: there are two questions we must ask if we wish to construct a sound logical basis for a Christian cosmogenesis that has real nobility. Is this progressive unification of the multiple in which creation consists as completely *free* and subordinate to God as we are to some degree obliged to assume it to be? Further, could it not correspond to an operation possible *only once* in divine history? The answers to these questions we may leave for the time being, and be satisfied with having established the following point: not only as a matter of fact in our own particular universe, but as a matter of logic which applies to every conceivable world (if a plurality of worlds is indeed possible), the creative act takes the form, for those beings which are its object, of transition from a state of initial dispersion to one of ultimate harmony. This remark will serve as a first step in correcting our idea of Christ's redemptive function; for it entails as a corollary a profound shift in our notion of the original Fall.

As we were saying earlier, a primary disorder cannot be justified in a world which is created fully formed: a culprit has to be found. But in a world which emerges gradually from

---

physically impossible for God to do: he cannot, for a start, make something past never to have existed. (Note by Père Teilhard.)

matter there is no longer any need to assume a primordial mishap in order to explain the appearance of the multiple and its inevitable satellite, evil. As for the multiple, it has, we have just seen, its natural place in the underlying basis of things, since, standing at the opposite pole from God, it represents the diffuse potentialities of participated being: not fragments of a broken pitcher, but the elemental clay from which everything will be moulded. And as for evil, this necessarily appears in the course of unification of the multiple, since it is precisely the expression of a state of plurality that is as yet incompletely organized. In the world which is in process of formation this transitory state of imperfection will no doubt be reflected, at the individual level, in a certain number of culpable acts. The very first examples of these (and the most decisive in human history, though the least conscious) may well be detached from the series and classed as a 'primary transgression'. But the original weakness from which the creature suffers is in reality the radical condition which causes it to be born from a starting-point in the multiple, always retaining in its fibres (until it is finally and permanently spiritualized) a tendency to fall back towards the bottom, into dust.

In these circumstances, evil is not an unforeseen accident in the universe. It is an enemy, a shadow which God inevitably produces simply by the fact that he decides on creation.[4] New being, launched into existence and not yet completely assimilated into unity, is a dangerous thing, bringing with it pain and oddity. For the Almighty, therefore, to create is no small matter: it is no picnic, but an adventure, a risk, a battle, to

4. Is not this precisely the truth adumbrated in all the myths in which the ideas of birth and evil are associated? We may say that all that would be needed to modernize Christology would be to clarify the notion of *sin*, as used in theological and liturgical formulas, by that of *progress*: in short, to explain smoke by fire. That is not asking much, surely? (Note by Père Teilhard.)

which he commits himself unreservedly. Can we not see what breadth and clarity is beginning to be added to the mystery of the Cross?

I say this with all sincerity: I have always found it impossible to be sincerely moved to pity by a crucifix so long as this suffering was presented to me as the expiation of a transgression which God could have averted – either because he had no need of man, or because he could have made him in some other way. '*Qu'allait-il faire dans cette galère?*'[5]

Seen, however, on the panoramic screen of an evolutive world which we have just erected, the whole picture undergoes a most impressive change. When the Cross is projected upon such a universe, in which struggle against evil is the *sine qua non* of existence, it takes on new importance and beauty – such, moreover, as are just the most capable of appealing to us. Christ, it is true, is still he who bears the sins of the world; moral evil is in some mysterious way paid for by suffering. But, even more essentially, Christ is he who structurally in himself, and for all of us, overcomes the resistance to unification offered by the multiple, resistance to the rise of spirit inherent in matter. Christ is he who bears the burden, constructionally inevitable, of every sort of creation. He is the symbol and the sign-in-action of progress. The complete and definitive meaning of redemption is *no longer only* to expiate: it is to surmount and conquer.[6] The full mystery of baptism is no longer to cleanse but (as the Greek Fathers fully realized) to plunge into the fire of the purifying battle 'for being' – no longer the shadow, but the sweat and toil, of the Cross.

5. i.e. (after Molière) 'What did he think he was up to?'

6. In view of the importance of anticipating oversimplified interpretations of this passage which distort the meaning, we have ourselves italicized *no longer only*. This is in order to make it quite clear that Père Teilhard is not denying the necessity of expiation when he includes it in a wider and more complex process of spiritual ascent, which itself depends on the expiation.

I fully appreciate the seriousness of the changes introduced by these new views. I am familiar with the solemn decrees of the Council of Trent on the subject of original sin. I am aware of the infinite network of formulas and attitudes through which the idea that we are the guilty children of Adam and Eve has percolated into our Christian life.[7]

Yet I beg my readers to reflect, calmly and impartially, on two things. The first is, that for all sorts of reasons – scientific, moral and religious – the classic *depiction* of the Fall has already ceased to be for us anything but a strait-jacket and a verbal imposition, the *letter* of which can no longer satisfy us either intellectually or emotionally. In its *material representation*, it no longer belongs either to our Christianity or to our universe. The second reason is that a transposition of the order of that which I suggest in no way interferes with, and even preserves all that is essential to, just that very reality and that urgent necessity in the Redemption which the Councils have sought to define. One simple change will be enough: we have only to say 'fire' where we have always spoken of 'smoke'.[8] The words are different but the thing is still the same. And, in the light of the new horizons history is opening up for us, I do not see how else we could preserve that thing or, *a fortiori*, ensure its triumph.

II. INCARNATION

Completely to adjust the idea of Redemption to the demands of evolution is an arduous task, even though it brings freedom with it. The figure of Christ emerges from the attempt with

7. On the author's progressive discovery of the truth of the Council's definitions, and their development, cf. *Vues Ardentes*, pp. 46-7 (Ed. du Seuil, Paris, 1967).

8. By purifying us, the Redemption makes us capable of loving, and Père Teilhard believes that it is time to give more emphasis in our thought to the fire of love rather than to the smoke.

added grandeur and beauty; but not without meeting resistance.

In the case of the idea of the Incarnation, things work out quite differently. When the face of Christ is projected, along the axis of this mystery, upon a universe that is evolutive in structure, it expands and fills out effortlessly. Within this organic and moving framework, the features of the God-man spread out and are amplified with surprising ease. There they assume their true proportions, as in their own natural context.

If we are to grasp the reason for this affinity and this successful projection, we must clearly understand what is meant by an evolutive world. It is one in which the consistence of the elements and their stability of balance lie in the direction not of matter but of spirit; in such a universe, we must remember, the fundamental property of the cosmic mass is to concentrate upon itself, within an ever-growing consciousness, as a result of attraction or synthesis. In spite of the appearance, so impressive as a factor in physics, of secondary phenomena of progressive dispersion (such as entropy), there is only one real evolution, *the evolution of convergence*, because it alone is positive and creative. There is no need for me to discuss this point again, for I have already dealt with it on several occasions elsewhere; but it has a consequence, of great importance for the Incarnation, to which I must return. It is this: quite apart from any religious consideration, we are obliged, by the very process of thought and experience, to assume the existence in the universe of a centre of universal confluence. As a structural necessity, if the cosmos is to hold together and progress, there must be in it a specially important place in which, as though at a universal crossroads, everything can be seen, can be felt, can be controlled, can be vitalized, can *be in touch* with everything else. Is not that an admirable place at which to position (or rather to recognize) Christ?

If we assume Christ to be established by his incarnation at this remarkable cosmic point of all convergence, he then immediately becomes co-extensive with the vastness of space. There is no longer any danger that his personality or his sovereignty may vanish, submerged in too enormous a universe. The dizzy immensities of the heavens no longer have any significance for our faith and our hope, if the countless beings which fill the ideal spheres are all embraced, through their centre, in a common infinity.

In such a position, again, Christ is commensurate with the abyss of time into which the roots of space are driven. We might have thought that his frail humanity would be lost in that abyss, taking our beliefs with it. But what value is, in fact, measured by the appearance in history of a life in a universe where the existence of the least monad is seen to be tied up with, and synchronous with, the whole evolution of things? The fact that Christ emerged into the field of human experience for just one moment, two thousand years ago, cannot prevent him from being the axis and the peak of a universal maturing.

In such a position, finally, Christ, wholly 'supernatural' though his domain may ultimately be, gradually radiates his influence throughout the whole mass of nature. Since, in concrete fact, only one single process of synthesis is going on *from top to bottom* of the whole universe, no element, and no movement, can exist at any level of the world outside the 'informing' action of the principal centre of things. Already co-extensive with space and co-extensive with duration, Christ is also automatically, in virtue of his position at the central point of the world, co-extensive with the scale of values which are spaced out between the peaks of spirit and the depths of matter.

Projected, then, on the screen of evolution, Christ, in an exact, physical, unvarnished sense, is seen to possess those most awesome properties which St Paul lavishly attributes to him. He is the First, and he is the Head. In him all things received their first impulse, in him all things hold together and all things are consummated. Once again, we might have feared that by immeasurably enlarging the limits of the world, science would make it more and more impossible to believe literally in that magnificent Pauline paean. And now we find that the contrary is true: it provides it with a perfect confirmation, so fine that we hardly dare to accept it. The greater the universe grows in our eyes, the more we see that it is made ready for unity. No, there is no danger that either 'height, breadth, or depth' can ever interpose between us and worship of Christ Jesus – provided that we have complete and final confidence in those immensities.

Without being unjust to the Latin Fathers, might one not blame them for having overdeveloped the rabbinical and legalistic side of St Paul in their theology? Under their influence the Christian history of the world has assumed the appearance of a legal trial between God and his creatures. Unmindful of a nobler tradition, our cosmology tended to be reduced to an argument about ownership, a humiliating and disheartening point of view.

The pressure of facts is now such that it is time to return to a form of Christology which is more organic and takes more account of physics. A Christ who is no longer master of the world solely because he has been *proclaimed* to be such, but because he animates the whole range of things from top to bottom; a Christ who dominates the history of heaven and earth not solely because these have been *given* to him, but because his gestation, his birth and gradual consummation constitute *physically* the only definitive reality in which the evolution of the world is expressed: there we have the only God whom we can henceforth worship sincerely. And that is precisely the God suggested to us by the new aspect the universe has assumed.

In all truth, we will be perfectly justified in saying that evolution has preserved our God for us if, through evolution, our religion is forced to recognize the existence of the universal

Christ and the fullness of his efflorescence. But to balance this (and this is even more true) we shall have to add that the universal Christ will have appeared just at the right time to protect the idea of evolution from itself.

At the point reached by its efforts scientifically and socially to build the world, mankind stands undecided. Analysis has taken the study of the earth's past and present as far as it can go. What now has to be done, following the cosmic currents revealed by history, is to confront the future; and that means, now that we have recognized evolution, to drive it further ahead. *All the spirit of the earth combining to produce an increase of thinking unity:* that is the avenue opening up ahead of us.

Confronted by the evidence for the necessity of this deliberate act, we go on talking but refuse to face the real issue. Why is this? Simply because we cannot bring ourselves to believe in the full truth of our discovery. Logically, we should have to admit that if the world is advancing towards the spiritual there must be a conscious peak to the universe. We cannot make up our minds to take the step involved in that admission. It is becoming clear that some impulse, real in order, must intervene to help us to get past this point of inertia. Why should not the world receive this jolt from Christians, from the people who live, by constant habit, in the feeling that beyond all outward appearances there lies a universal centre of reflective action? The Church (and this is perhaps the clearest evidence of her immortal truth) is alone now in effectively preserving the idea and the experience of a *personal Godhead*. We must delay no longer in securing for this faith a real inherent sovereignty in the domain of natural spiritual constructions.

If, as we hope, Christ one day triumphs over the modern world, we shall owe this victory to the fact that he will be what we may well call the saviour of evolution: he will save it both by his existence (which alone can reveal to us historically the cosmic centre called for by the general theory of the universe), and, as we still have to explain, by his gospel (which alone can transform us into faithful servants of the advancing world).

III. THE GOSPEL MESSAGE

'There has been too much talk of lambs. Give the lions a chance.' Too much gentleness and not enough force. Those symbols are a fair summary of my feelings and my theme, as I turn to the question of readjusting the gospel teaching to the modern world.

This question is vital. The great majority of our contemporaries have no distinct interest in the meaning to be attached to the mysteries of the Incarnation and the Redemption. All, however, react sharply to the interior effects of agreement or disagreement which they produce for them in the field of morality and mysticism. We Christians often flatter ourselves that if so many Gentiles still fight shy of the Faith it is because the ideal we hold up for their admiration is too perfect and too difficult. This is an illusion. A noble difficulty has always fascinated souls. The truth about today's gospel is that it has ceased, or practically ceased, to have any attraction because it has become *unintelligible*. In a world which has been so awesomely modified, the same words are being repeated to us as served our fathers. *A priori*, it would be a safe bet that these antique expressions can no longer satisfy us.[9] In fact, the best non-believers I know would feel that they were falling short of their moral ideal if they went through the gesture of conversion: they have told me so themselves.

Here again, if we are to remain faithful to the gospel, we have to adjust its spiritual code to the new shape of the universe. Henceforth the universe assumes an additional dimension for our experience. It has ceased to be the formal garden from which we are temporarily banished by a whim of the Creator.

9. Unless interpreted in the light of the present dimensions of the world.

It has become the great work in process of completion which we have to save by saving ourselves. We are finding out that we are the elements responsible, at the atomic level, for a cosmogenesis. Transferred into this new space, what becomes of Christian moral rules of conduct? How are they to accommodate themselves if they are still to remain themselves?

One sentence will serve as an answer: By becoming, for God, the reinforcement of evolution. Hitherto the Christian was brought up under the impression that he could attain God only by abandoning everything. He is now discovering that he cannot be saved except through the universe and as a continuation of the universe. There was a time when the gospel teaching could be summed up in the words of the Epistle: '*Religio munda haec est: visitare pupillos et viduas, et immaculatum se custodire ab hoc saeculo.*'[10] That time is gone for ever; or rather, the words of St James must be interpreted with the full moral depth that new horizons enable us to see in them.

To worship was formerly to prefer God to things, relating them to him and sacrificing them for him. To worship is now becoming to devote oneself body and soul to the creative act, associating oneself with that act in order to fulfil the world by hard work and intellectual exploration.

To love one's neighbour was formerly to do him no injury and to bind up his wounds. Henceforth charity, without losing any of its compassion, will attain its full meaning in life given for common progress.

To be pure was formerly to hold oneself aloof from, to guard against, contamination. The name of chastity will be given tomorrow primarily to sublimation of the powers of the flesh and of all passion.

To be detached was formerly to attach no value to things, and to abstain from them, as far as possible. To be detached

10. 'Religion that is pure and undefiled . . . is this: to visit orphans and widows . . . and to keep oneself unstained from the world' (James 1:27).

will become more and more to leave behind every truth and every beauty in turn, precisely in virtue of the love one has for them.

To be resigned could formerly mean passive acceptance of present conditions in the universe. Resignation will now be confined to the wrestler capitulating in the grip of the angel.

It used to appear that there were only two attitudes mathematically possible for man: to love heaven or to love earth. With a new view of space, a third road is opening up: to make our way to heaven *through* earth. There is a communion (the true communion) with God through the world; and to surrender oneself to it is not to take the impossible step of trying to serve two masters.

Such a Christianity is still in reality the true gospel teaching, since it represents the same force applied to the elevation of mankind above the tangible, in a common love.

Yet, at the same time, this teaching has no taint of the opium which we are accused with such bitterness (and not without justification) of dispensing to the masses.

It is no longer, even, simply the soothing oil poured into the wounds of mankind, the lubrication for its labouring mechanism.

The truth is that it comes to us as the animator of human action, to which it offers the clear-cut ideal of a divine figure, discernible in history, in which all that is essentially most precious in the universe is concentrated and preserved.

It provides the exact answer to all the doubts and aspirations of an age suddenly woken into consciousness of its future.

This presentation of the gospel, and this alone, so far as we can judge, stands out as capable of justifying and maintaining in the world the fundamental zest for life.

It is the very religion of evolution.

Some years ago, in the course of a conversation with an old missionary – something of a visionary, but universally regarded as a saint – I heard him make the following surprising statement: 'History shows that no religion has been able to maintain itself in the world for more than two thousand years. Once that time has run out, they all die. And it is coming up to two thousand years for Christianity . . .' By that he, as a prophet, meant that the end of the world was close at hand; but to me his words had a graver import.

Two thousand years, more or less, is indeed a long stage for man particularly if, as is happening today, there has just been added to it the critical point of a 'change of age'. So many attitudes and outlooks are modified after twenty centuries that, in the context of religion, we have to slough off the old skin. Our formulas have become narrow and inflexible; we find them irksome, and they have ceased to have an emotional impact on us. There must be a 'moult' if we are to continue to live.

As a Christian, I am barred from believing that it is possible for Christianity to disappear in this period of transition that is upon us, as has happened to other religions. I believe Christianity to be immortal. But this immortality of our faith does not prevent it from being subject (even as it rises above them) to the general laws of periodicity which govern all life. I recognize, accordingly, that at the present moment Christianity (exactly like the mankind it embraces) is reaching the end of one of the natural cycles of its existence.

By dint of repeating and developing in the abstract the expression of our dogmas, we are well on the way to losing ourselves in the clouds where neither the turmoil nor the aspirations nor the living vigour of the earth can penetrate. Religiously, we are living, in relation to the world, in a twofold intellectual and emotional isolation: an indication that the time for a renewal is close at hand. After what will soon be two thousand years, Christ must be born again, he must be reincarnated in a world that has become too different from that in which he lived. Christ cannot reappear tangibly among us; but he can reveal to our minds a new and triumphant aspect of his former countenance.

I believe that the Messiah whom we await, whom we all without any doubt await, is the universal Christ; that is to say, the Christ of evolution.

Unpublished, Tientsin, Christmas 1933. Printed from a copy bearing a manuscript note 'Revised and corrected' followed by the signature 'Teilhard'.

HOW I BELIEVE

This paper was written by Père Teilhard in answer to a request from Mgr. Bruno de Solages, characteristic of the latter's deep concern for the apostolate.

I believe that the universe is an evolution.
I believe that evolution proceeds towards spirit.
I believe that spirit[1] is fully realized in a form of personality.
I believe that the supremely personal is the universal Christ.

LIKE every other form of human knowledge, religious psychology is built upon experience. It needs facts. And since the circumstances are such that the facts occur only at the deepest level of men's consciousness, this branch of knowledge cannot develop until individuals supply the necessary 'confessions'.

It is entirely with this sort of documentary purpose in mind that I have tried to pin down, in what follows, the reasons for my faith as a Christian, with the shades of emphasis it bears, and also its limitations or difficulties. I in no way believe that I am better or more important than any other man: it simply happens that for a number of accidental reasons my own case is significant, and on that ground it is worth recording.

The originality of my belief lies in its being rooted in two domains of life which are commonly regarded as antagonistic. By upbringing and intellectual training, I belong to the 'children of heaven'; but by temperament, and by my professional studies, I am a 'child of the earth'. Situated thus by life at the

1. 'Today, I would say, "I believe that *in man*, spirit is fully realized in person."' (Note added by Père Teilhard, in 1950, in *Le Cœur de la Matière*.)

heart of two worlds with whose theory, idiom and feelings intimate experience has made me familiar, I have not erected any watertight bulkhead inside myself. On the contrary, I have allowed two apparently conflicting influences full freedom to react upon one another deep within me. And now, at the end of that operation, after thirty years devoted to the pursuit of interior unity, I have the feeling that a synthesis has been effected naturally between the two currents that claim my allegiance. The one has not destroyed, but has reinforced, the other. Today I believe probably more profoundly than ever in God, and certainly more than ever in the world. On an individual scale, may we not see in this the particular solution, at least in outline, of the great spiritual problem which the vanguard of mankind, as it advances, is now coming up against?

I am going to broadcast the seed, and let the wind carry it where it will. Let me say again, these pages make no claim to determine the theory of a general apologetics. All I am proposing to do is to describe, so far as I understand them, the developments of a personal experience. As such, what I have to say will not satisfy everybody. Any particular reader may well find it difficult to accept this or that fact which I quote in evidence, with a consequent break in the logical continuity of the terms of my argument.

Nevertheless, it remains true that, expressed in forms that are infinitely varied, there can ultimately be only one psychological axis of spiritual progress towards God. Even if they are expressed in completely subjective terms, many of the things I am going to say must necessarily have their equivalents in temperaments different from my own – and they must raise a sympathetic echo in them. Man is essentially the same in all of us, and we have only to look sufficiently deeply within ourselves to find a common substratum of aspirations and illumination. To put it in a way which already expresses my fundamental thesis: 'It is through that which is most incommunicably personal in us that we make contact with the universal.'

INTRODUCTION: THE EVOLUTION OF FAITH

On the strictly psychological plane to which I intend to confine myself here, I mean by 'faith' any adherence of our intelligence to a general view of the universe. We may try to define this adherence by certain aspects of freedom ('option') or of affectivity ('appeal') which accompany it, but those seem to me derived or secondary characteristics. In my view, the essential note of the psychological act of faith is to perceive as possible, and accept as more probable, a conclusion which, in spatial width or temporal extension, cannot be contained in any analytical premises. *To believe is to effect an intellectual synthesis.*

Proceeding from that assertion, it seems to me that the first condition imposed by our experience upon every object, if it is to be *real*, is not that it remains always identical with itself, nor, on the contrary, is constantly changing – but that it grows while still retaining certain dimensions proper to itself which cause it to be *continually homogeneous with itself*. All around us, every life is born from another life, or from a 'pre-life'; every freedom is born from another freedom, or from a 'pre-freedom'. Similarly, I maintain, in the domain of beliefs, *every faith is born from a faith*. This form of birth, it is true, does not exclude reasoning. Just as freedom emerges in nature by gaining control of determinisms and building upon them, so faith advances in our minds by weaving around itself a coherent network of thoughts and action; but this network grows and holds together ultimately only under the organizing influence of the initial faith. This is necessitated by the principle of homogeneity, transposed into religious psychology, which governs the synthetic transformations of nature.

To believe is to develop an act of synthesis whose first origin is inapprehensible.

It follows from this twofold proposition that, if I am to demonstrate my Christian faith to myself, I cannot have (nor, in fact, have I ever found) any other way of doing so than by verifying in my own self the legitimacy of a psychological evolution. In a first phase, I feel the need to descend, step by step, to ever more elementary beliefs, until I reach a certain fundamental intuition below which I can no longer distinguish anything at all. In a second phase, I try to re-ascend the natural series (I was on the point of saying 'phylum') of my successive acts of faith in the direction of an over-all view which ultimately is found to coincide with Christianity. First one has to verify the solidity of an inevitable initial faith, and then one has to verify the organic continuity of the successive stages which the augmentations of that faith pass through. I know no other apologetics for my own self and I cannot therefore suggest any other to those for whom I wish the supreme happiness of one day finding themselves face to face with a unified universe.

PART ONE
THE INDIVIDUAL STAGES OF MY FAITH

1. *Faith in the World*

If, as the result of some interior revolution, I were to lose in succession my faith in Christ, my faith in a personal God, and my faith in spirit, I feel that I should continue *to believe* invincibly *in the world*. The world (its value, its infallibility and its goodness) – that, when all is said and done, is the first, the last, and the only thing in which I believe. It is by this faith that I live. And it is to this faith, I feel, that at the moment of death, rising above all doubts, I shall surrender myself.

How can one describe, and how can one justify this fundamental adherence?

In its most deeply buried form, faith in the world (as I experience it) is seen in a particularly live sense of universal
relationships of interdependence. A certain philosophy of the
continuum has sought to set up the intellectual fragmentation
of the world against the progressive advances of mysticism.
In my own self, things work out differently. The more one
heeds the invitations to analyse urged on one by contemporary thought and science, the more one feels imprisoned
in the network of cosmic interrelationships. Through criticism
of knowledge, the subject becomes continually more closely
identified with the most distant reaches of a universe which
it can know only by becoming to some degree one body
with it. Through biology (descriptive, historical, and experimental), the living being becomes more and more in
series with the whole web of the biosphere. Through physics,
a boundless homogeneity and solidarity is brought to light in
the layers of matter. 'Everything holds together.' Expressed in
this elementary form, faith in the world does not differ notice-
ably from the acceptance of a scientific truth. It appears in a
certain predilection for probing deeper into a fact (the fact of
universal interrelationship) which nobody questions, and in a
certain tendency to give this fact precedence over the other
fruits of experience. And it is, I believe, under the combined
influence of this appeal and this 'slant' that the decisive step in
the birth of my faith is taken. For every man who thinks, the
universe forms a system endlessly linked in time and space. By
common agreement, it forms *one bloc*. In my view that word
is no more than an approximation, notionally over-fluid; it
must inevitably be carried to its conclusion in a more decisive
term – the world constitutes a *whole*. Is the transition from the
first concept to the second justified? And in what form of
perception is it effected?

It is essential to note that in this emergent state the idea of the Whole is still extremely vague in my mind and to all appearance ill-defined. Is it a static totality we are concerned with, or a dynamic? Is it material or spiritual? Is it progressive in its movement, or is it periodic and circular? These are questions with which I am not yet concerned. It is simply that, above the complete linked body or ensemble of beings and phenomena, I can glimpse, or sense, a global reality whose condition is that of being more necessary, more consistent, richer and more certain in its ways, than any of the particular things it embraces. For me, in other words, there are no longer any 'things' in the world; there are only 'elements'.

One hardly notices the transition from 'ensemble' to 'whole', or from 'things' to 'elements'; carry it only a little further and we might speak of their 'identity'. However, it is just at this point, in fact, that we meet an initial split in the thinking mass of mankind. The classification of intelligences or souls seems as though it must be an impossible task. In reality, it obeys an extremely simple law. Beneath an infinite number of secondary differentiations, caused by the diversity of social interests, of scientific investigations or religious faiths, there are basically two types of mind, and only two: those who do not go beyond (and see no need to go beyond) perception of the multiple – however interlinked in itself the multiple may appear to be – and those for whom perception of this same multiple is necessarily completed in some unity. There are only, in fact, pluralists and monists: those who do not see, and those who do. Are these two opposite tendencies, in those whom they affect, congenital and in consequence unalterable, and is one justified in saying of one of them that it is the 'true' one? Here we have in embryo the whole problem of the absolute value of faith, and of the possibility of conversion.

The most convenient solution (and the one that many people adopt, in fact, as a way out) consists in saying that it is simply a matter of taste and 'temperament'. A man is born a monist or a pluralist, as he is born a geometrician or a musician. There is nothing 'objective' to be found behind either of the two attitudes. They are simply an expression of our instinctive preferences for one or other of two points of view equally offered by the universe.

This answer seems to me an evasion of the problem.

In the first place, there is no real equivalence, if we really think about it, between the two confronting terms. To be a pluralist is like being a fixist; in both cases the words cover a void, or a lack. Basically, the pluralist adopts no positive attitude. All he does is to decline to give any explanation. He must, therefore, either deny any sort of superiority to the *positive* over the *negative*, or he must, necessarily, come down on the side of the only constructive possibility open for us: to treat the universe as though it were one.

Is there, however, any need to speak of the *force of necessity* in these questions? Does not the presence of the Whole in the world assert itself for us with the direct evidence of some source of light? I do indeed believe that that is so. And it is precisely the value of this primordial intuition which seems to me to hold up the whole edifice of my belief. Ultimately, and in order to account for facts which I have met at the deepest level of my consciousness, I am led to the conclusion that man, in virtue of his very condition of 'being in the world', possesses a special *sense* which shows him, in a more or less ill-defined way, the Whole of which he forms a part. There is nothing astonishing, after all, in the existence of this 'cosmic sense'. Because he is endowed with sex, man undoubtedly has intuitions of love. Because he is an element, surely he must in some obscure way feel the attraction of the universe. In fact, nothing in the vast and polymorphous domain of mysticism (religious, poetical, social and scientific) can be explained without the hypothesis of such a faculty, by which we react synthetically to the spatial and temporal ensemble of things in order to apprehend the Whole behind the multiple. You may, if you wish, speak of 'temperament', since the cosmic sense, like all the other intellectual qualities, has degrees of liveliness and penetrative power that vary with the individual. But it is an *essential* temperament, in which the structure of our being is as necessarily expressed as it is in the desire to extend one's being and to attain unity. I said earlier that there are two basic categories of mind, pluralist and monist, but I must now correct that statement. Individually, the 'sense of the Whole' may be atrophied, or may well lie dormant. Matter, however, could more easily be immune to gravity than a soul could be to the presence of the universe. By the very fact that they are men, even pluralists could have the power of 'seeing'. They are monists without realizing it.

Later, carried along by the logic of my own development, I shall return to a consideration of the comforting mass of human religious thought which consciously operates in the passionately felt attraction of the Whole; and I shall look to this mighty primordial current to give me the ultimate orientation about which my personal thought is undecided. For the moment it is enough for me to have the assurance of the value of a profoundly felt personal intuition, based on an almost universal agreement.

I surrender myself to an ill-defined faith in a world that is one and infallible – wherever it may lead me.

2. *Faith in Spirit*

Everything we look at takes on more exact definition. This general law of perception holds good for the cosmic sense. We cannot have aroused ourselves to consciousness of the Whole without the initially vague contours of universal reality tending, as we grope our way, to take on form. Up to this point, I have the impression that the birth of my faith was an almost organic phenomenon, almost a reflex, like the eyes' response to light. I can now distinguish, in the progress of my world vision, the intervention of factors which are more clearly linked with my own time, upbringing and personality.

A first point which emerges for me with a forcefulness that I cannot even dream of questioning, is that the unity of the world is by nature dynamic or evolutive. Here I am simply meeting in myself, in a participated and individual form, the discovery of duration, which for the last century has so profoundly been modifying mankind's former consciousness of the universe. Besides space, so staggering to Pascal, we now have time – not a container-time in which years are stored, but an organic time which is measured by the development of global reality. We used to look upon ourselves and the things around us as 'points', closed in on themselves. We now see beings as like threadless fibres, woven into a universal process. Everything falls back into a past abyss, and everything rushes forward into a future abyss. Through its history, every being is co-extensive with the whole of duration; and its ontogenesis is no more than the infinitesimal element of a cosmogenesis in which is ultimately expressed the individuality – the face, we might say – of the universe.

Thus the universal Whole, like each element, is defined for me by a particular movement which animates it. When, however, I ask what sort of movement this can be and whither it is taking us, my decision is reached by my feeling suggestions and indications, gathered in the course of my professional researches, working inside my mind and falling into a pattern: and it is as an historian of life, at least as much as a philosopher, that I answer, from the depths of my intelligence and of my heart, 'Towards spirit'.

Spiritual evolution. I know that the juxtaposition of these two words still seems contradictory, or at any rate anti-scientific, to a great number (and perhaps the majority) of natural scientists and physicists. Because research into evolution shows us that we must attach, step by step, states of higher consciousness to antecedents which are apparently inanimate, we have to a great extent succumbed to the *materialist illusion*. This consists in regarding the elements of analysis as 'more real' than the terms of synthesis. At this moment, it could well appear that the discovery of time had thrown down the dykes behind which a static philosophy protected the transcendence of 'souls', and was thereby washing away spirit in floods of material particles. Spirit no longer existed – there was nothing but matter. I am convinced that this retrogression has been halted and that henceforth, carried along by the same evolutionary current, we are again rising up towards converse concepts: matter no longer exists, there is nothing but spirit.

In my own particular case, the 'conversion' was effected through study of the 'fact of man'. It is a curious thing: man, the centre and creator of all science, is the only object which our science has not yet succeeded in including in a homogeneous representation of the universe. We know the history of his bones: but no ordered place has yet been found in nature for his reflective intelligence. In the midst of a cosmos in which primacy is still accorded to mechanisms and chance, thought – the redoubtable phenomenon which has revolutionized the earth and is commensurate with the world – still appears as an inexplicable anomaly. Man, in that part of him which is the most human, is still, as an achievement, a monstrous stumbling-block.

It was in order to avoid this paradox that I decided to reverse the elements of the problem. If we start from matter, and express man on that basis, he becomes the unknown quantity of an insoluble equation. Why not, then, express him as a known term of the real? Man appears to be an exception. Why not, then, make him the key of the universe? Man refuses to allow himself to be forced into a mechanistic cosmogony. Why not, then, construct a physics whose starting-point is spirit? For my own satisfaction, I tried this approach to the problem. And it suddenly seemed to me that reality was vanquished and lay disarmed at my feet.[2]

The first result of simply making a change in the variable quantity was that the whole of life on earth took on form. So long as one insists on distributing the mass of living beings simply according to anatomical details, they spread out in countless different directions without any regular order; but as soon as we look for the expression of a constant drive towards a higher degree of spontaneity and consciousness, then the whole readily falls into position; and thought finds its natural place in this development. Supported by an infinite number of organic gropings, the thinking animal ceases to be an exception in nature; it simply represents the highest embryonic stage we know in the growth of spirit on earth. At one bound, man found himself placed on a principal axis of the universe. I then found, by an almost inevitable generalization of this initial observation, that even wider vistas were opening

2. If one is to carry out this simple act, which is at the same time an act of release, one must, it is evident, overcome the *illusion of quantity*. Man seems pitifully lost and accidental in the immensities of stellar space. But is it not the same with radium, through which our views on matter have been revolutionized? We have also to overcome the *illusion of fragility*. Man, the latest comer among animals, would appear to be held up in the world only by a pyramid of exceptional circumstances: but have we not the whole history of the earth to assure us that nothing progresses more infallibly in nature than the improbable syntheses of life? Finally, we must not allow ourselves to be intimidated by the accusation of *anthropocentrism*. We are told that it is childish vanity for man to solve the problem of the world in terms of himself. But is it not a scientific truth that in the field of our experience there is no thought but man's thought? Is it our fault that we coincide with the central axis of things? Could it, moreover, be otherwise, since we are endowed with intelligence? (Note by Père Teilhard.)

up for me. If man is the key to the earth, surely the earth must, in turn, be the key to the world. On earth we perceive a constant increase in *psyche* throughout time. May not this great law be the most general expression we can arrive at of universal evolution? An evolution which is material in basis leaves no place for man, for all the accumulation of determinisms still cannot provide even a shadow of freedom. On the other hand, an evolution with a basis of spirit preserves all the laws noted by physics, while at the same time leading directly to thought; for a mass of elementary freedoms, subject to no order, amounts to a determinism. Such an evolution preserves *both* man and matter: and must therefore be accepted.

It was when I realized how successful was this approach that 'faith in spirit' was finally and fully realized in my mind. The principal articles of that faith may be expressed as follows:

a. The unity of the world presents itself to our experience as the over-all ascent towards some continually more spiritual state, of a consciousness that is initially pluralized (and as though materialized). My complete and impassioned adherence to this fundamental proposition is essentially synthetic in order. It results from a gradual and harmonious organization of all that knowledge of the world contributes to me. No other formula seems to me sufficient to cover the whole of experience.

b. Precisely in virtue of the condition which defines it (that is, its appearance as the term of universal evolution) the spirit in question has a special, well-defined nature. It in no way represents some entity which is independent of matter or antagonistic to it,[3] some force locked up in, or floating in, the physical world. By spirit I mean 'the spirit of synthesis and sublimation', in which is painfully concentrated, through end-

---

3. Matter is used here in its immediate and concrete sense (to denote the physical world), and not in its learned (philosophical or mystical) sense of the *anti-spiritual aspect* of beings. (Note by Père Teilhard.)

less attempts and setbacks, the potency of unity scattered throughout the universal multiple: *spirit which is born within, and as a function of matter.*

c. The practical corollary of this outlook is that, to guide him through the fog-banks of life, man has an absolutely certain biological and moral rule, which is continually to direct himself 'towards the greater degree of consciousness'. If he does this, he can be certain of sailing in convoy and making port with the universe. In other words, we should use the following as an absolute principle of appraisal in our judgments: 'It is better, no matter what the cost, to be more conscious than less conscious.' This principle, I believe, is the absolute condition of the world's existence. And yet many, in fact, contest it, implicitly or explicitly, without any idea of the enormity of their denial. On very many occasions, after some fruitless discussion on advanced points in philosophy or religion, I have suddenly heard my companion say that he did not see that a human being was absolutely higher than a Protozoan – or, again, that progress is a bad thing for nations. Our controversy had been built upon a fundamental lack of knowledge. For all his learning, my friend had not understood that the only reality in the world is the passion for growth. He had not taken the elementary step without which all that I still have to say will seem illogical and unintelligible.

3. *Faith in Immortality*

When I had reached the level of faith in a spiritual evolution of the world, I felt the temptation (as many others have felt it before me, I imagine) of stopping at that point. Is there, I wondered, any need to go beyond that vision of hope in order to find a basis for a moral attitude to life, and to justify and purify that life? And yet, once again, as a result of contemplating the universe with sympathy and admiration, I felt my belief evolving within me; and I realized that the discovery in and around me of a nascent spirit meant nothing at all if that spirit were not immortal. Immortality which, in the very wide sense in which I use the word, means *irreversibility* – it was that which seemed to me to be the consequence, as a necessary property or complement, of any idea of universal progress.

That the universe, *as a whole*, cannot ever be brought to a halt or turn back in the movement which draws it towards a greater degree of freedom and consciousness, was originally suggested to me by the very nature of spirit. In itself, spirit is a constantly increasing physical magnitude; there is, indeed, no discernible limit to the depths to which knowledge and love can be carried. But if spirit *can* grow greater without any check, surely that is an indication that it *will* in fact *do so* in a universe whose fundamental law would appear to be 'if a thing is possible, it will be realized'. In fact, as far back into the past as our experience can penetrate, we can see throughout the ages a continual rise of consciousness. We may discuss endlessly whether human intelligence has yet gained anything, in the course of history, in individual perfection; but one thing is certain – that in the short interval covered by the last two centuries, the *collective* powers of spirit have increased to an impressive degree. All around us there is a general convergence, and everything is on the point of forming one solid bloc within mankind. Today we may say truthfully and without leaving the field of facts, that the world we live in is drifting, as far as the eye can reach, under the pull of two combined opposite currents, each equally irreversible: entropy and life.

The evident impossibility of life (taken as a whole) to fall back is already a solid argument in favour of belief in what spirit has won, and in its indestructibility. This demonstration is nevertheless open to the objection that it belongs to the empirical order, and that, in short, it applies only to a limited area and phase of the universe. It would be much more satisfactory to attach 'immortality' directly to some essential property of cosmic evolution. Let us see whether we can do so.

For a long time now, I have thought that I have found the solution of this problem, to my own satisfaction, in analysis of 'action'. To act (that is to say, to apply our will to the realization of some progress) would appear to be so simple a thing that it requires no explanation. In reality, however, we find the same in connexion with this elementary function as we find with external perception. From the 'commonsense' point of view, seeing, hearing and feeling used to appear to be directly intelligible acts. Nevertheless, their justification has called for immense critical effort, at the end of which it has become apparent (as we were recalling earlier) that each one of us to some degree forms but one with the totality of the universe. It is the same with action. We act, true enough – but what structural properties must the real possess if it is to be possible for this movement of the will to be effected? What conditions must the world satisfy if it is to be possible for a conscious freedom to operate in it? Following Blondel and Le Roy, the answer I give to this problem of action is: 'If that thing, apparently so small, which we know as human activity, is to be set in motion, nothing less is required than the attraction of a result that cannot be destroyed. We press on only in the hope of an immortal conquest.' And from this I draw the direct conclusion that 'ahead of us there must therefore lie something that is immortal'.

Let us examine in turn the major premise and the middle term of this argument.

First, the major: this seems to me to represent an elementary psychological fact, even though to perceive it calls for a certain training of the inner eye. For my own part, the thing is clear: in the case of a *true act* (by which I mean one to which one gives something of one's own life), I cannot undertake it unless

I have the underlying intention (as Thucydides noted many centuries ago) of constructing 'a work of abiding value' – not, of course, that I am so vain as to wish to bequeath my name to posterity, but some sort of essential instinct makes me guess at the joy, as the only worthwhile joy, of co-operating as one individual atom in the final establishment of a world: and *ultimately nothing else can mean anything to me*. To release some infinitesimal quantity of the absolute, to free one fragment of being, for ever – everything else is but intolerable futility.

I have often made myself question the value of this interior evidence. Numbers of my friends have assured me that they have experienced nothing of the same sort themselves. 'It is a matter of temperament', they have told me. 'You feel the need to philosophize. But why rationalize one's tendencies? We simply get on with our work and studies because that is what we like doing, just as we have a drink.' And, being certain that I have seen deep inside myself an essentially human, and there-fore universal, characteristic, I answer them, 'You are not searching to the full depth of your heart and mind. And that, moreover, is why the cosmic sense and faith in the world are dormant in you. You find satisfaction in the fight and the victory, and it is there that the attraction lies. But can you not see, then, that what is satisfied in you by effort is the passion *"for being finally and permanently more"* – would it be the same if some day (no matter how distant) *nothing* were to remain of your work, for *anybody*? In its present form, your zest for life is still emotional and weak. I seem to you peculiar and exceptional because I am trying to analyse my own zest and to relate it to some structural feature of the world. And I tell you, in all truth, that before the human mass sets out tomorrow on the great adventure from which its fulfilment is to emerge, it must gather itself together, as one whole, and once and for all investigate the value of the drive which is urging it ahead. Is it really worth our while to yield – or even, as we must do, to devote ourselves passionately – to the forging ahead of the world? Man, the more he is man, can give himself only to what he loves; and ultimately he loves only what is indestructible. Multiply to your hearts' content the extent and duration of progress. Promise the earth a hundred million more years of continued growth. If, at the end of that period, it is evident that the whole of consciousness must revert to zero, *without its secret essence being garnered anywhere at all*, then, I insist, we shall lay down our arms – and mankind will be on strike. The prospect of a *total death* (and that is a word to which we should devote much thought if we are to gauge its destructive effect on our souls) will, I warn you, when it has become part of our consciousness, immediately dry up in us the springs from which our efforts are drawn. Consider all around you the increasing number of those who are privately bored to tears and those who commit suicide in order to escape from life ... The time is close at hand when mankind will see that, precisely in virtue of its position in a cosmic evolution which it has become capable of discovering and criticizing, it now stands biologically between the alternatives of suicide and worship.'

However, if the major premise of my argument is true – if, that is, not by whim but by internal necessity, 'reflective life' can proceed only in the direction of the immortal – then, *given the stage which I am presupposing the evolution of my faith has reached*, I am justified in concluding, as I have done, that 'the immortal therefore exists'. And, indeed, if the world, taken as one whole, is something infallible (first stage); and if, moreover, it moves towards spirit (second stage); then it must be capable of providing us with what is essentially necessary to the continuation of such a movement. By this I mean it must provide *ahead of us an unlimited* horizon. Without this, the world would be incapable of sustaining the progress it stimulates, and would be in the inadmissible situation of having to wither away in apathy every time the consciousness born in it reached the age of reason.

It was thus that the mirage of matter finally faded from my sight. I too, and I perhaps more than anybody, at first privately located in the mass of physical objects the universe's point of balance and principle of consistence. Gradually, however, under the pressure of facts, I witnessed a reversal of the values. The world does not hold together 'from below' but 'from above'. Nothing is seemingly more unstable than the syntheses gradually effected by life. And yet it is in the direction of these fragile constructions that evolution advances, never to fall back.

When everything else, after concentrating or being dissipated, has passed away, spirit will remain.

4. *Faith in Personality*

You see, then, how by degrees my initial faith in the world was irresistibly transformed into a faith in the increasing and indestructible spiritualization of the world. In fact, this point of view is simply that to which the majority of monist-type minds more or less vaguely conform. It would, indeed, be difficult otherwise to respect 'the phenomenon of man'. But when we come to consider in what form we should picture to ourselves the immortal term of universal evolution, we find differences of belief. Ask a monist[4] how he sees the universe's ultimate spirit. Nine times out of ten he will answer, 'As a vast impersonal force in which our personalities will be engulfed'. The conviction which I wish to defend here is the exact converse of this; it is that if there is life ahead of us, and irreversibly so, this living being must culminate in a personal being in which we are to be 'super-personalized'. How do I justify this new stage in the unfolding of my faith?

4. I am using the word, of course, as meaning the opposite of 'pluralist', and not in a Hegelian sense. (Note by Père Teilhard.)

Once again, I do so simply by obeying the suggestions that come to me from the real, holding together throughout itself in harmony as one entire whole.

The idea, now so prevalent, that the Whole, even when reduced to the form of spirit, cannot but be impersonal, undoubtedly originates in a *spatial illusion*. The 'personal' with which we are constantly in contact is an 'element' (a monad); on the other hand it is primarily by diffuse activities that the universe is made known to our experience. This accounts for the persistent impression that person is exclusively an attribute of the particular as such – and that it must, in consequence, grow less as total unification is effected.

However, at the point I reached in the development of my faith, this impression does not stand up to intellectual examination. The spirit of the world, in the nascent form in which it appeared to me, is not a fluid, an ether, or an energy. It is completely different from any such nebulous materiality; it is a gradual acquisition of consciousness in which life's countless achievements are associated together organically in their essence. I defined it earlier as 'spirit of synthesis and sublimation'. By what analogical road, then, can we form an image of it? Certainly not as a relaxation of our individual reflective and affective centre, but rather as a concentration of that centre, carrying that process always further beyond it. 'Personalized' being, which makes us to be *human*, is the highest state in which we are enabled to apprehend the stuff of the world. Carried to its fullest development, this substance must already contain, to a supreme degree, all that is most valuable in our perfection. It cannot, therefore, but be 'super-conscious', which means 'super-personal'. You may jib at the idea of a personal universe; the association of these two concepts may seem to you grotesque; but this, let me repeat, is a spatial illusion. Instead of looking at the cosmos in the aspect presented by its external, material sphere, turn back to the point at which all the radii meet. There too, brought back to unity, the Whole exists – and you can apprehend it in its entirety, concentrated at that point.

Thus, for my own part, I cannot conceive an evolution towards spirit which does not culminate in a supreme personality. The cosmos cannot, as a result of its convergence, be knit together in *some thing*; it must, as already happens in a partial and elementary way in the case of man, end upon *some one*. Then, however, we meet the complementary question of what will remain of each one of us in this ultimate consciousness of itself which the universe will attain.

In itself, to be frank, the problem of personal survival does not worry me greatly. Once the fruit of my life has been gathered up into an immortality, a self-centred consciousness of that fact or enjoyment of it matters little to me. I can say in all sincerity that my personal happiness means nothing to me. It is enough for me in that respect that what is best in me should pass, there to remain for ever, into one who is greater and finer than I.

Yet, it is from the very essence of my indifference to survival that the necessity of survival forces itself on my attention. I spoke of 'what is best in me'; but what, then, is this precious fragment which the Whole is waiting to harvest in me? Is it an idea developed in my thought? a word I have spoken? a light I have radiated? . . . In that respect, it is clear, I am sadly lacking. Let us admit that I am one of those rare human beings whose visible trace does not disappear like the wake of a ship; let us admit, too, and make the fullest possible allowance for the part – a very real part – played by the imponderable influences that every living being unwittingly exercises on the universe around him. But what does this fraction of my applied energy represent in comparison with the focus of thought and affectivity constituted by 'my soul'? My life's work, it is true, is in some way represented by that part of me which passes into all my fellows; but it is much more fully represented by what I succeed in producing, deep within myself, that is incommunicable and *unique*. My personality, that is, the particular centre of perceptions and love that my life consists in developing – it is that which is my real wealth. And in that, accordingly, lies the only value whose worth and whose preservation can call for and justify my effort. And in that, again, consists the supreme portion of my being which cannot be abandoned by the centre in whom all the sublimated treasures of the universe converge.

We see, then, that this transmission of my self to the other is demanded both by the requirements of my action and by the successful fulfilment of the universe. How is it to be effected? Must I strip myself of what is 'me' and give it to 'him'? It would appear that we sometimes feel that such a gesture is possible; but we have only to reflect for a moment to realize that this is an illusion; and we shall then recognize that our personal qualities are not a flame from which we can cut ourselves off by handing it on to another. We thought, maybe, that we could divest ourselves of them, as we take off a coat and give it away. In fact, however, these qualities coincide with the substance of our being, for they are woven in their fibres by the consciousness we have of them. What must be retained in the consummation of the universe is nothing less than the *properties of our centre*: and it is accordingly this centre itself – it is precisely that by which our thought is reflected on itself – which must be saved. The reality in which the universe culminates cannot be developed from a starting-point in ourselves, unless in so doing it preserves us. It must be that in the supreme personality we shall inevitably find ourselves personally immortalized.

You may find this an astonishing prospect: but that is because the materialist illusion is still at work, in one of its many forms, and it is leading you astray, as it has led astray the majority of pantheists. We almost inevitably, as I recalled at the beginning of this section, picture the great Whole to ourselves as a vast ocean in which the threads of individual being disappear. It is the sea in which the grain of salt is dissolved, the fire in which the straw goes up in smoke. Thus to be united with that great Whole is to be lost. But what I want to be able to proclaim to all men is that this is a false picture, and contradicts everything that has emerged most clearly in the course of my awakening to faith. The Whole is not, definitely not, the tensionless, and thus dissolving, immensity in which you look for its image. Like us, it is essentially a centre, possessing the qualities of a centre. Now, what is the only way in which a centre can be formed and sustained as such? Is it by breaking down the lower centres which fall under its governance? Indeed it is not – it is by strengthening them in its own image.[5] Its own particular way of dissolving is to carry unification still further. For the human monad, fusion with the universe means super-personalization.

It is at this point that the individual developments of my faith come to a stop and culminate at a point at which, were I to lose confidence in all revealed religion, I would still, I believe, be firmly anchored. Stage by stage, my initial faith in the world has taken a definite shape. What was at first a vague intuition of universal unity has become a rational and well-defined awareness of a presence. I know now that I belong to the world and that I shall return to it, not simply in the ashes of my body, but in all the developed powers of my mind and heart. *I can love the world.* And since, therefore, I can now distinguish in the cosmos a higher sphere of person and per-

5. Which amounts to saying that true union (that is spiritual union, or union in synthesis) differentiates the elements it brings together. This is no paradox, but the law of all experience. Two beings never love one another with a more vivid consciousness of their individual selves than when each is swallowed up in the other. (Note by Père Teilhard.)

sonal relationships, I am beginning to suspect that appeals and indications of an intellectual nature may well build up around me and have a message for me.

A presence is never dumb.

PART TWO

THE CONFLUENCE OF RELIGIONS

1. *The Religious Phenomenon and the Choice of Religion*

Precisely in virtue of the unitary and convergent structure we have already recognized in the universe, the lines of development followed by my belief in the course of its individual stages cannot be a single isolated thread in the evolution of human thought. If it is true that the Whole reveals itself to each of its elements in order to draw it to itself – and if it is also true that all self-conscious activity organically experiences the need to vindicate to itself the value of its effort – then the birth of my faith represents no more than an infinitesimal element of a vastly wider and more certain process, common to all men. And thus it is that I find myself obliged by the very logic of my progress to emerge from my individualism and confront the general religious experience of mankind, *that so I may involve myself in it.*

There are, I know, many minds, with an interior sensitivity to the divine, which shrink from this act of adherence to an external compulsion to believe. Religion is a strictly personal matter; that is what the most intelligent of us think, or are prepared to think. From the spiritual-evolutionary point of view to which faith in the world has led me, I have already implicitly condemned this individualist claim. To my mind, the religious phenomenon, taken as a whole, is simply the reaction of the universe as such, of collective consciousness and human action in process of development.[6] At the social level, it expresses the passionate faith in the Whole which I thought to distinguish in my own self. This, surely, can mean only one thing – that there cannot be any subject other than the totality of thought on earth. Religion, born of the earth's need for the disclosing of a god, is related to and co-extensive with, not the individual man but the whole of mankind. In religion, as in science, is accumulated, and given proper direction, and gradually and infallibly organized, an infinity of human inquiries. How could I fail to associate myself with that accumulation; and where else could I find what confirms and complements the personal process which has brought me secretly to the feet of a presence who calls for my worship but has not yet spoken? I would not be so foolish as to seek to build up science by my own un-aided efforts. Similarly, my own effort to reach faith can suc-ceed only when contained within a total human experience and prolonged by it. I must therefore plunge resolutely into the great river of religions into which the rivulet of my own private inquiries has just flowed. Yet when I look around me, I see that the waters are disturbed; the eddies are whirling in so many different directions. From so many quarters I can hear the summons of this or that divine revelation. To which of these apparently opposed currents am I to surrender my-self, if the stream is to carry me to the ocean?

In all the old apologetics, the choice of religion was princip-ally governed by the consideration of the miraculous. The privileged position of a doctrine that it could offer itself with an array of powers 'superior to the forces of nature', guaranteed

6. Nothing, accordingly, is more mistaken than the view that religion is a primitive and transitory stage through which mankind passed in its infancy. The more man becomes man, the more will it be necessary for him to be able to, and to know how to, worship. The religious phenomenon is only one of the aspects of 'hominization'; and, as such, it represents an irreversible cosmic magnitude. (Note by Père Teilhard.)

its coming from God. No one but the Creator could make use of this seal of warranty. In consequence, once the miracle had been established, an extremely simple syllogism made it plain that all men had to do was to accept the guidance provided by the wonder-worker, *no matter how much*, apart from that, they were attracted or repelled by the prospect of conforming to it. It was, of course, assumed that the word of God could not but be both intellectually and emotionally satisfying to his creature. The fact, however, and the function of this harmony between our desires and revelation were mostly left as an implication.

Personally, I have no difficulty in accepting miracles, providing (and this, in fact, is precisely what the Church teaches) the miracle does not run counter to the *continually more numerous and exact* rules we are finding in the natural evolution of the world.[7] I may say even more: convinced as I am that the determinisms of matter are no more than the remnants of spirit's period of bondage, I would find it impossible to accept that a progressive liberation of physical bodies should not be found (and to a greater degree than elsewhere) closely associated with the main axis of spiritualization which the 'true religion' represents. Yet, precisely because this continual upward shifting of the limits of our possibilities seems to me to constitute an unbroken continuation of a natural property of evolution, I can no longer see it as characterized by a break, amounting to a divine rending of the seamless veil of phenomena. Properly understood, the miracle is still a criterion of truth for me, but it is a subordinate and secondary criterion. The only reason that can decide me to adhere to a religion must, in short (as follows from the first part of this essay), consist in the harmony of a higher order which exists between that

7. In fact, taking even the gospel marvels in the form they are often presented in, I feel obliged to admit that I believe not because of but in spite of the miracles I am offered. And I am sure that that is the unacknowledged position of a great many Christians. (Note by Père Teilhard.)

religion and the individual creed to which the natural evolution of my faith has led me.

Faith in the unity of the world, faith in the existence and faith in the immortality of the spirit which is born from the synthesis of the world – these three faiths, summed up in the worship of a personal and personalizing centre of universal convergence – these, let me say once more, are the terms of that creed. Let us see to which current I must commit myself if these aspirations are to find the warmest welcome, are to be rightly directed, and are to multiply. It is in this that, for me, the test of religions will consist.

2. Religions Put to the Test

In spite of certain superficial proliferations, for which the dissatisfaction of the faithful is more responsible than the birth of a new ideal, the complex of religions is tending, under the influence of the 'modern' spirit, towards a remarkable simplification. That is at any rate the impression I gain from observing them. And since I am explicitly concerned here only with my own self, I shall say that in my view a first inspection is sufficient to reduce types of *possible* belief to three: the group of Eastern religions, the humanist neopantheisms, and Christianity. These are the three signposts between which I might hesitate, were I (as I am here hypothetically supposing) in the position of still in real fact having to choose my religion.[8]

a. The great appeal of the *Eastern religions* (let us, to put a name to them, say Buddhism) is that they are supremely

8. Islam, in spite of the number of its adherents and its continual progress (in the less evolved strata of mankind, we may note) is not examined here, because to my mind (at least in its original form) it contributes no special solution to the modern religious problem. It seems to me to represent a residual Judaism, with no individual character of its own: and it can develop only by becoming either humanist or Christian. (Note by Père Teilhard.)

universalist and cosmic. Never perhaps has the sense of the Whole, which is the life-blood of all mysticism, flowered more exuberantly than in the plains of India. It is there, when a synthetic history of religions comes to be written, that we shall have to locate, some centuries before Christ, the birth of pantheism. It is there again, when the expectation of a new revelation is growing more intense, that in our days the eyes of modern Europe are turned. Governed, as I have described, by love of the world, my own individual faith was inevitably peculiarly sensitive to Eastern influences; and I am perfectly conscious of having felt their attraction, until the day came when it became clear to me that by the same words the East and I understood different things. For the Hindu sage, spirit is the homogeneous unity in which the complete adept is lost to self, all individual features and values being suppressed. All quest for knowledge, all personalization, all earthly progress are so many diseases of the soul. *Matter is dead weight and illusion.* By contrast, spirit is for me, as I have said, the unity by synthesis in which the saint realizes his full being, carrying to the furthest possible point what differentiates its nature, and the particular resources it possesses. Knowledge and power – that is the only road that leads to freedom. *Matter is heavily loaded, throughout, with sublime potentialities.* Thus the East fascinates me by its faith in the ultimate unity of the universe; but the fact remains that the two of us, the East and I, have two diametrically opposed conceptions of the relationship by which there is communication between the totality and its elements. For the East, the One is seen as a suppression of the multiple; for me, the One is born from the concentration of the multiple. Thus, under the same monist appearances, there are two moral systems, two metaphysics and two mysticisms.[9] Once the

9. I am speaking here, of course, of the Eastern religions as they should rightly be regarded in virtue of their fundamental concept of spirit, and not in the form they assume in fact in the varieties of neo-Buddhism, under the

ambiguity is made plain, no more will be needed I think (since Eastern religions logically lead to passive renunciation) for our modern world, eager as it is to find above all a religious vindication for its achievements, to reject them. For me, in any case, their current has *ipso facto* lost its power. The God whom I seek must reveal himself to me as a saviour of man's work. I thought that I could discern him in the East. But it is clear that he awaited me at the other end of the horizon in those areas more recently opened to human mysticism by the 'road of the West'.

b. Unlike the venerable cosmogonies of Asia which I have just dismissed, the *humanist pantheisms* represent in our world an extremely youthful form of religion. It is a religion which (apart from Marxism) as yet knows little or no codification, a religion with no apparent god, and with no revelation. But it is a religion in the true sense of the word, if by that word we mean contagious faith in an ideal to which a man's life can be given. In spite of many differences in detail, a rapidly increasing number of our contemporaries are henceforth agreed in recognizing that the supreme value of life consists in devoting oneself body and soul to universal progress – this progress being expressed in the tangible developments of mankind. It is a very long time since the world has witnessed such an effect of 'conversion'. This, surely, can only mean that in forms that vary (communist or nationalist, scientific or political, individual or collective) we have without any doubt been watching for the last century the birth and establishment of a new faith: the religion of evolution. This is the second of the two spiritual currents against which I have to measure my faith.

By nature and profession I am (as I remarked earlier) too

---

influence of an approximation to Western types of mysticism. (Note by Père Teilhard.)

much a child of the world not to feel at home in a temple built to the glory of the earth. And what in truth is the 'cosmic sense' from which germinates the whole organism of my faith, but precisely this same faith in the universe which animates modern pantheisms? I rejected the East because it left no logical place or value for the developments of nature. In humanisms, on the other hand, I find the genesis of the greatest measure of consciousness, with its essential accompaniment of creation and research of every kind, erected into a sort of absolute. In this I see a stimulation to unlimited efforts to conquer time and space. This, I feel, is the natural interior climate in which I am made to develop and evolve. I can find no other explanation for the immediate sympathy and profound agreement I have always noted between myself and the most emancipated servants of the earth. I have often been beguiled, accordingly, by dreams of venturing in their footsteps, curious to discover how far our paths might coincide. But on each occasion, I have very soon been disappointed. What I found was that after a fine start the worshippers of progress immediately come to a halt, without the desire or ability to go beyond the second stage in my individual belief. They set out eagerly, it is true, towards faith in spirit (the *true* spirit of sublimation and synthesis), but at the same time they hold back from investigating whether, to justify the gift they make of themselves, this spirit must be seen by them as endowed with immortality and personality. Much more often than not they deny it these two properties, which, in my view, are essential to the justification of man's effort; or, at any rate, they try to build up the body of their religion without reference to those properties. This very soon produces a feeling of insecurity, of incompleteness, and of suffocation.

The Hindu religions gave me the impression of a vast well into which one plunges in order to grasp the reflection of the sun. When I turn to the humanist pantheisms of today I feel that the lowering sky is pressing down on me and stifling me.

c. All that I can do, then, is to look to the third and last branch of the river – the *Christian current*. By a process of elimination it is clear that this is the direction I am seeking – where I shall meet, amplified by a long living tradition, the tendencies from which my faith emerged and by which it is maintained. I surrendered myself, accordingly, to the influences of the Church. And this time it was not by the fiction of an intellectual experience but in the course of a prolonged concrete effort that I tried to make my own petty personal religion coincide with the great religion of Christ. Well, if I am to be absolutely *true* to myself as to others, I must admit that for a third time I did not succeed in establishing agreement – at least at the outset. At first, I did not recognize myself in the gospel: and for a reason I shall explain.

Christianity is eminently the religion of the imperishable and the personal. Its God thinks, loves, speaks, punishes, rewards, in the same way as *a person* does. The universe of Christianity culminates in immortal souls, eternally responsible for their own destiny. Thus, over the heads of its faithful, the same heaven opens up with a wide welcome, as for the pantheists remained impassive and closed. There is a magnificent power of attraction in this illumination of the peaks; but, I thought for a long time, the road to reach them had no connexion with the earth – as though I had been asked to scale the clouds. The reason for this was that, as a result of seeing only 'personal' relationships in the world, the average Christian has ended by reducing the creator and creature to the scale of 'juridical man'. In his effort to exalt the value of spirit and supernaturality of the divine, he has come to look upon the soul as a transient guest in the cosmos and a prisoner of matter. For such a Christian, accordingly, the universe has ceased to extend the primacy of its organic unity over the whole field of interior experience: the operation of salvation, reduced to being no more than a matter of personal success, develops without any reference to cosmic evolution. Christianity gives the impression of not believing in human progress. It has never developed *the sense of the earth*, or it has allowed that sense to lie dormant in it ... No wonder, then, that I – I, whose very life-blood is drawn from matter – felt that my adherence to the morality and theology of Christianity was forced and conventional. Faith in Christ fulfils my highest hopes, the very hopes which neither the pantheisms of the East nor those of the West could satisfy. But it does so, I thought, only, with the other hand, to take away from me the one spring-board from which I could rise up to the expectation of a divine immortality – it robs me of faith in the world. And so I had a new question to answer: does my individual religion make such novel and exceptional demands that no older formula can satisfy them?

I feared that this might well be so.

It was then that the universal Christ was revealed to me.

3. *The Universal Christ and the Convergence of Religions*

The universal Christ, as I understood the name, is a synthesis of Christ and the universe. He is not a new godhead – but an inevitable deployment of the mystery in which Christianity is summed up, the mystery of the Incarnation.

So long as it is described and treated in juridical terms, the Incarnation appears a simple phenomenon – one that can be superimposed upon any type of world. Whether the universe be large or small, static or evolutionary, it is equally simple for God to *give* it to his Son: for all that is involved, to put it briefly, is a declaration. A very different situation comes to light if we look at it from an organic point of view, which is basically the point of view of all true knowledge of the real. The Christian's (or rather, to be more precise, the Catholic's) dearest belief is that Christ envelops him in his grace and makes him participate in his divine life.[10] When we go on to ask by what physical possibility this mysterious process is effected, we are told 'by the divine power'. Very well – but this is no more an answer than is the negro's who explains an aircraft by saying 'white man's magic'. How exactly is the divine power to put the universe together in such a way that it may be possible for an incarnation to be biologically effected in it? That is what matters to me, and that is what I tried to understand. And my search led me to the following conclusion.

If we Christians wish to *retain* in Christ the very qualities on which his power and our worship are based, we have no better way – no other way, even – of doing so than fully to accept the most modern concepts of evolution. Under the combined pressure of science and philosophy, we are being forced, experientially and intellectually, to accept the world as a coordinated system of activity which is gradually rising up towards freedom and consciousness. The only satisfactory way of interpreting this process (as I added earlier) is to regard it as irreversible and convergent. Thus, ahead of us, a *universal cosmic centre* is taking on definition, in which everything reaches its term, in which everything is explained, is felt, and is ordered. It is, then, in this physical pole of universal evolution that we must, in my view, locate and recognize the plenitude

10. This higher union is effected, we are also told, in a 'supernatural' zone of the soul. And the theologian seems to imagine that by adding this obscure qualification he is excused from investigating how the demands of dogma and the potentialities of the earth may be reconciled with one another. Nevertheless, the problem remains, and it is an extremely serious problem. Whatever may be the precise positive content of the term 'supernatural', it cannot mean anything except 'supremely real', in other words 'supremely in conformity' with the conditions of reality which nature imposes on beings. If, then, Christ is to be *able* to be the saviour and the life of souls in their supernatural developments, he must first satisfy certain conditions in relation to the world, apprehended in its experiential and natural reality. (Note by Père Teilhard.)

of Christ. For *in no other type of cosmos*, and *in no other place*, can any being, *no matter how divine he be*, carry out the function of universal consolidation and universal animation which Christian dogma attributes to Christ.[11] By disclosing a world-peak, evolution makes Christ possible, just as Christ, by giving meaning and direction to the world, makes evolution possible.

I am only too well aware how staggering is this idea of a being capable of gathering up all the fibres of the developing cosmos into his own activity and individual experience. But, in conceiving such a marvel, all I am doing (let me repeat) is to transpose into terms of physical reality the juridical expressions in which the Church has clothed her faith. In just the same way, the humblest Catholic unwittingly, through his creed, imposes a particular structure on the universe. It is a fantastic but a coherent story: for, as I pointed out earlier, is it not a mere quantitative illusion which makes us regard the personal and the universal as incompatible?

For my own part, I set out resolutely in the only direction in which it seemed to me possible to carry my faith further, and so retain it. I tried to place at the head of the universe which I adored from birth, the risen Christ whom others had taught me to know. And the result of that attempt has been that I have never for the last twenty-five years ceased to marvel at the infinite possibilities which the 'universalization' of Christ opens up for religious thought.

Judging from first appearances, Catholicism disappointed me by its narrow representations of the world and its failure to understand the part played by matter. Now I realize that, on the model of the incarnate God whom Christianity reveals to me, I can be saved only by becoming one with the universe. Thereby, too, my deepest 'pantheist' aspirations are satisfied,

11. In other words, Christ needs to find a world-peak for his consummation, just as he needed to find a woman for his conception. (Note by Père Teilhard.)

guided, and reassured. The world around me becomes divine. And yet the flames do not consume me, nor do the floods dissolve me. For, unlike the false monisms which urge one through passivity into unconsciousness, the 'pan-Christism' which I am discovering places union at the term of an arduous process of differentiation. I shall become the Other only by being utterly myself. I shall attain spirit only by bringing out the complete range of the forces of matter. The total Christ is consummated and may be attained, only at the term of universal evolution. In him I have found what my being dreamed of: a personalized universe, whose domination personalizes me. And I hold this 'world-soul' no longer simply as a fragile creation of my individual thought, but as the product of a long historical revelation, in which even those whose faith is weakest must inevitably recognize one of the principal lines of human progress.

For (and this is perhaps the most wonderful part of the whole story) the universal Christ in whom my personal faith finds satisfaction, is none other than the authentic expression of the Christ of the gospel. Christ renewed, it is true, by contact with the modern world, but at the same time Christ become *even greater in order* still to remain the same Christ. I have been reproached as being an innovator. In truth, the more I have thought about the magnificent cosmic attributes lavished by St Paul on the risen Christ, and the more I have considered the masterful significance of the Christian virtues, the more clearly have I realized that Christianity takes on its full value only when extended (as I find it rewarding to do) to cosmic dimensions. Inexhaustibly fructified by one another, my individual faith in the world and my Christian faith in Christ have never ceased to develop and grow more profound. *By this sign*, which argues a continual agreement between what is most determinedly emergent in me and what is most alive in the Christian religion, I have finally and permanently recognized that in the latter I have found the complement I sought to my own self, and to that I have surrendered.[12]

But, if I have thus surrendered myself, why should not others, all others, also do the same? I began by saying that what I am now writing is a personal confession. Deep in my mind, however, as I have proceeded, I have felt that something greater than myself was making its way into me. The passion for the world from which my faith springs; the dissatisfaction, too, which I experience at first when I am confronted by any of the ancient forms of religion – are not both these traces in my heart of the uneasiness and expectancy which characterize the religious state of the world today?

In the great river of mankind, the three currents (Eastern, human and Christian) are still at cross-purposes. Nevertheless there are sure indications which make it clear that they are coming to run together. The East seems already almost to have forgotten the original passivity of its pantheism. The cult of progress is continually opening up its cosmogonies ever more widely to the forces of spirit and emancipation. Christianity is beginning to accept man's effort. In these three branches the same spirit which made me what I am is obscurely at work.

In that case, surely the solution for which modern mankind is seeking must essentially be exactly the solution which I have come upon. I believe that this is so, and it is in this vision that my hopes are fulfilled. A general convergence of religions upon a universal Christ who fundamentally satisfies them all: that seems to me the only possible conversion of the world, and the only form in which a religion of the future can be conceived.

12. The more I think about it, the less I can see any criterion for truth other than the establishment of a growing maximum of universal coherence. Such an achievement has something *objective* about it, going beyond the effects of *temperament*. (Note by Père Teilhard.)

EPILOGUE
THE SHADOWS OF FAITH

I have finished detailing the reasons for my faith and the different forms in which it has been expressed. All I have now to do is to tell you what sort of clarity and security I find in the outlook I have accepted: and then I shall have completed the history of my faith.

From what I have just said about my conviction that there is a divine personal term to universal evolution, it might be thought that, stretching ahead of my life, a bright and serene future can be distinguished. For my part, it is assumed, death appears simply as one of those periods of sleep after which we can count on seeing the dawn of a glorious new day.

The reality is very different.

Certain though I am – and ever more certain – that I must press on in life as though Christ awaited me at the term of the universe, at the same time I feel no special assurance of the existence of Christ. Believing is not seeing. As much as anyone, I imagine, I walk in the shadows of faith.

The shadows of faith: to justify this dimness – so strangely incompatible with the sunlight of the Godhead – the doctors of the Church explain that the Lord deliberately hides himself from us in order to test our love. One would have to be irretrievably committed to mental gymnastics, one would have never to have met in one's own self or in others the agonies of doubt, not to feel the hatefulness of this solution. With your own creatures, God, standing before you, lost and in torment, clamouring for help – and when all you have to do to make them hasten to you would be to let one glance from your eye fall on them, to show them just the fringe of your garment – can I believe that you would not do so?

To my mind, this penumbra of faith is simply a particular case of the problem of evil. And I can see only one way of overcoming this *fatal* stumbling-block. This is to recognize that if God allows us to suffer, to sin, to doubt, it is because he *cannot* here and now cure us and show himself to us. And, if he cannot do so, it is exclusively because we are still *incapable*, by reason of the present phase of the universe, of a higher degree of organization and illumination.

Evil is inevitable in the course of a creation which develops within time. Here again the solution which brings us freedom is given us by evolution.

No: God, I am quite certain, does not hide himself so that we shall have to look for him – any more than he allows us to suffer in order to increase our merit. On the contrary, reaching out to the creation which is making its way up to him, he works with all his strength to beautify and illuminate it. Like a mother, he watches over his latest-born. But my eyes cannot yet see him. Will it not, in fact, call for the whole duration of the centuries before our sight is attuned to the light?

Our doubts, like our misfortunes, are the price we have to pay for the fulfilment of the universe, and the very condition of that fulfilment. That being so, I am prepared to press on to the end along a road in which each step makes me more certain, towards horizons that are ever more shrouded in mist.[13]

That, then, is how I believe.

Peking, 28 October 1934.

13. The mists were later to clear. 'For four months now the sun of Christic energy has been steadily climbing to the zenith in my sky (intellectual and mystical).' So Père Teilhard was to write in 1947 to his friend the Abbé Gâté.

And Père Teilhard's last writings evidence the climax of illumination: 'It is in the blaze of a universal translucence and a universal conflagration that I shall know the bliss of closing my eyes' (*Le Cœur de la Matière*, 1950).

'Energy transforming itself into presence . . . It would appear that a single ray of such a light, falling upon the noosphere, would inevitably produce an explosion powerful enough instantaneously to set ablaze and refashion the face of the earth' (*Le Christique*, March 1955).

SOME GENERAL
VIEWS ON THE ESSENCE
OF CHRISTIANITY

1. In its essence, Christianity consists in regarding the history of the world as corresponding to the following process: A supreme I (or Me), a hyper-personal God, incorporates in itself, without destroying their identity, the human 'I's', in and through the 'Christic I'.

2. *The attitude expressed in practice* by this point of view is unmistakable, and is seen historically to possess an unrivalled – we might almost say limitless – evolutive mystical value.

3. The problem presented by the construction of a *static rational scheme* which retains both the relative independence and at the same time the organic interdependence of these three categories of 'I', has produced a complicated metaphysical theology (theory of persons, of nature in God and in Christ).

4. In a *dynamic form*, the Christian point of view can be expressed quite clearly by the symbolic diagram overleaf. The multiple (created) converges gradually towards unity (in God), the apex of the cone being formed by Christ, in whom the unified plural (the organized sum total of created centres of consciousness) meets the active centre of unification.

N.B. As a further detail, note, in the symbolic 'cone', the section across the 'hominization' surface, where the multiple reaches the state of reflective consciousness. It is at this critical surface (appearance of man) that the centres or grains of consciousness can first be regarded as definitely constituted (i.e. it is only from that point that the created 'I's' are constituted).

5. Adopting this dynamic point of view (in which creation

THE DIVINE

Universal Christ

Historic Christ

S . . . . S

S.S.—Hominization-surface
on which the granules of
created personality appear.

is presented essentially in terms of evolution) it is important
to observe that *the same* fundamental process can be called
creation, incarnation, or redemption, according to what aspect
of it is considered:

a. Creation, in as much as the secondary 'I's' (the human
'I's') are constituted under the magnetic influence of the
Divine 'I'.

b. Incarnation, in as much as the operation is effected through
unification; thus the Divine 'I', as a direct result of its own
operation, cannot but 'immerse' itself in its work.

c. Redemption, in as much as, at whatever point *during* the
process of unification the created is considered, it represents a
portion of residual non-organization or disorganization (actual
or potential) which is the determining factor in all forms of
evil. In one sense, if to create is to unite (evolutively, gradually)
then God cannot create without evil appearing as a shadow –

evil which has to be atoned for and overcome. This is not a limitation on God's power, but the expression of a law of nature, an ontological law, which it would be illogical to suppose God could contravene.

N.B. This, incidentally, broadens, without distorting, the 'meaning of the Cross' to a remarkable degree. The Cross is the symbol and significant act of Christ raising up the world with all its burden of inertia, but with all its inherent drive, too; an act of expiation but one also of breakthrough and conquest. Creation belongs to the category of 'effort'.

6. From this it follows that, understood in their full sense, creation, incarnation and redemption are not facts which can be *localized* at a given point in time and space; they are true dimensions of the world (not objects of perception, but a condition of all possible perceptions).

It is nevertheless true that all three can take the form of particular *expressive* facts, such as the historical appearance of the human type (creation), the birth of Christ (incarnation), his death (redemption). These historical facts, however, are only a specially heightened expression of a process which is 'cosmic' in dimensions.

Similarly, I have no difficulty in accepting that the evil inherent in the world as a result of its method of creation can be regarded as becoming specially individualized on earth simultaneously with the appearance of responsible human 'I's'. This would be the original sin, in the *strict sense* of the word, of the theologians.[1] In another sense one might wonder whether the true human sin might not be the sin of man who later attained a sort of fullness of his consciousness and responsibility.[2]

1. From the theological point of view one cannot overlook the cardinal importance of such a proposition.

2. Cf. above, 'Note on Some Possible Historical Representations of Original Sin,' p. 53, n. 5.

7. What gives Christianity its peculiar effectiveness and sets it in a particular key, is the fundamental idea that the supreme focus of unity is not only reflected in each element of consciousness it attracts, but also, in order to produce final unification, has had to 'materialize' itself in the form of an element of consciousness (the Christic, historical 'I'). In order to act effectively, the centre of centres reflected itself on the world in the form of a centre (=Jesus Christ).

When first entertained, this concept of Christ not only as prophet and man exceptionally conscious of God, but as 'divine spark', is abhorrent to the modern mind, as being an outworn anthropomorphism. But it should be noted:

a. That the modern reaction against anthropomorphism has gone much too far, to the point of making us doubt a divine ultra-personality. If we recognize that the true universal (the centre of the universe) cannot, by nature, but be hyperpersonal, then its historical manifestation in a personal form becomes logically comprehensible again, subject to correcting certain of our representations in detail.

b. Secondly, that psychologically, in fact, the astonishing power of mystical development displayed by Christianity is indissolubly linked with the idea that Christ belongs to history. Once this central core is removed, Christianity becomes no more than a 'philosophy' no different from the others; it loses all its force and vitality.

8. From the point of view we are adopting here, Christianity would appear fully to satisfy the essential religious tendency which impels man towards some sort of 'pantheism'.

There are two sorts of pantheisms:

a. Those for which the unity of the whole is born from fusion of the elements – as the former appears, so the latter disappear.

b. Those for which the elements *are fulfilled* by entering a deeper centre which dominates them and super-centres them

in itself. In virtue of the principle (both theoretic and experiential) that union does not confuse the terms it unites, but
differentiates them, the second form of 'pantheism' is the only
one which is intellectually justifiable and mystically satisfying.

It is precisely this latter form which is expressed in the
Christian attitude.

9. It is a common reproach against Christianity that it is
out of date because based on both an anthropomorphism (of
God) and an anthropocentrism (of man).

No one could deny that at a particular period of history
there was, for obvious reasons, a tendency for the nature of
the divine 'I' and the significant (privileged) position of man to
be conceived in terms that were oversimplified and over-
human. Such representations were much too summary, of
course, but they did contain an enduring substratum of truth.

If, indeed, we regard God no longer as an ordinary centre
of consciousness (human in type) but as a *centre of centres*;
and if we regard man no longer as the centre of the world but
as an axis (or leading shoot) pointing in the direction in which
the world is advancing (towards an ever higher degree of
consciousness and personality) – then we avoid the weaknesses
of anthropomorphism and anthropocentrism, and yet retain
all the requirements of Christian dogma; simply by a richly
rewarding change of dimensions.

Unpublished, Paris, May 1939.

CHRIST THE EVOLVER,
OR A LOGICAL DEVELOPMENT OF
THE IDEA OF REDEMPTION[1]

Henceforth the world will be able to make the sign of the cross only with a cross that has become a symbol of growth at the same time as of redemption.

Introductory Note
   I. A New Prospect in Science: Humanization
  II. An Apparent Conflict in Christian Thought: Salvation and Evolution
 III. A Coming Theological Advance: The Creative Aspect of Redemption
Final Observation
Appendix: Original Sin and Evolution

INTRODUCTORY NOTE

What follows is not written for the general public, but only for professionals. In the past I have been open to the reproach of having imprudently disseminated views whose novelty might well disturb and mislead minds that are ill-equipped to accommodate or appraise them. In this essay I am not addressing the great mass of believers or non-believers, in an attempt to open up for them a boundlessly enlarged field of worship: I am writing for my fellow philosophers and theologians, in the hope of awakening them to consciousness of a state of

1. Reflections on the nature of Christ's 'formal action' in the world.
Cf. Bonsirven: Rap. (Jewish historical concept)=constitution of the *Messianic era* (a concept which appears *after* Egypt). (Note by Père Teilhard.)

affairs which they, I am sure, can deal with more effectively than I can – but which, for various reasons, I am perhaps in a position to distinguish more clearly than they.

I mean the increasing necessity we are experiencing today of readjusting the fundamental lines of our Christology to a new universe.

I. A NEW PROSPECT IN SCIENCE: HUMANIZATION

If the theoreticians of Christianity wish to use language that is intelligible and (what is even more important) convincing to our contemporaries, one thing, above all, is indispensable: they must understand and accept with real sympathy, the new ideas of himself which modern man has been *scientifically* obliged to develop.

At an initial stage, this idea is one of an organic and genetic dependence which links mankind intimately with the rest of the world. *Man is born, and grows, historically, in dependence on the whole of matter and the whole of life.* I agree that this point has not as yet been fully appreciated by traditional philosophy and theology; but these difficulties and delays (inherent in every reorientation of thought) in no way alter a situation whose *definitive* character must be intellectually grasped by the 'teachers in Israel'. Using the word 'evolution' in its most generally accepted meaning, and in a purely experiential context, I would say that man's origin by way of *evolution* is now an *indubitable* fact for science. There can be no two ways about it: the question is settled – so finally that to continue to debate it in the schools is as much a waste of time as it would be to go on arguing whether or not the revolution of the earth is an impossibility.

While we continue to fight a rearguard action against what are henceforth established facts, the scientific problem of man is not standing still: without waiting for us, it has already moved into a second stage, which is a natural development and a completion of the first.

The nineteenth century and the early years of the twentieth were primarily concerned to throw light on man's *past* – the result of their inquiries being to make it unmistakably clear that the appearance of thought on earth corresponded biologically to a *'hominization' of life*. We are now finding that the concentration of scientific researches, focused *ahead* on the extensions of the 'phenomenon of man', is opening up an even more astonishing prospect in that direction: that of a *progressive 'humanization' of mankind*.

Let me explain what I mean.

Hitherto we have been tending instinctively to picture mankind as being bounded above by a sort of surface of evaporation (death), through which souls, the successive products of generations, escape one by one – and vanish. This system remains in a state of equilibrium, and includes no cycle more extensive than that of individual lives. Understood in this way, mankind would perpetuate itself on earth, and even extend itself, throughout the ages, but without any change in its level.

A very different picture begins to emerge when we look at it with eyes that are now accustomed to the vastness and the slowness of cosmic movements.

As seen by modern anthropology, the human group no longer forms a static aggregate of juxtaposed elements, but constitutes a sort of super-organism, subject to a global and well-defined law of growth. Man (and in this he resembles every other living thing) was born not only as an individual, but also *as a species*. It is appropriate, accordingly, to recognize and study in him, beyond the cycle of the individual, *the cycle of the species*.

Scientists are still a long way from reaching agreement about the particular nature of this higher cycle. I do not think that I would be mistaken, however, in saying that the idea is gaining ground in scientific circles, and will soon be generally accepted, that the biological process now taking place in mankind consists, specifically and essentially, in the progressive development of a collective human consciousness. It is becoming continually more evident that the general phenomenon of life can be reduced, biochemically, to the gradual building up of ultra-complex, and in consequence ultra-organized, molecular groupings. *Through its axial, living, portion, the universe is drifting, simultaneously and in just the same way, towards the super-complex, the super-centred, the super-conscious.*

From this point of view (upon which all modern physics, chemistry and biology converge, and which sums them all up) the phenomenon of man assumes for the first time a determinate and coherent significance in nature. In the past, we see the human individual standing at the head of animal life, with the supreme complexity and perfect centricity of his nervous system; and, in the future, we see at the head of hominized life the formation we can now expect of a higher grouping (of a type as yet unknown on earth) in which all human individuals will be at the same time completed and synthesized.

Thus each of our own particular 'ontogeneses' is included in a general anthropogenesis, in which the essence of cosmogenesis is probably expressed.

This prospect will seem wildly fantastic to those of my readers who have not made themselves familiar with the now indisputable vastness of the depths in which modern scientific thought is imperturbably developing.

Let me repeat and emphasize that, substantially, this view does no more than express what everyone is beginning to suspect and what everyone will be thinking tomorrow – to the utmost peril (some feel) or the utmost benefit (others, including my own self, feel) of our religion.

II. AN APPARENT CONFLICT IN CHRISTIAN THOUGHT:
SALVATION AND EVOLUTION

So long as they involved only the structure of matter or the vastness of space, the most recent scientific advances could be effected without any special repercussion on the peace of mind of believers. The relationship between the sensational revelations of the immense and the minute and the dogmatic teaching of the gospel was not sufficiently direct to be felt immediately. When we come to 'humanization' it is a very different story. Here we have a new compartment or rather an additional dimension; and suddenly this compartment and dimension, of which *there is no explicit mention in the gospel*,[2] intervenes and enlarges man's destiny almost limitlessly. Hitherto the Christian had been taught to think, to act, to fear and to worship, *on the scale of his own individual life and death*. How can one expect him, without breaking through the framework of tradition, to expand his faith, his hope and his charity to the measure of a terrestrial organization which is destined to continue throughout millions of years?

There is a lack of proportion between the insignificant mankind still presented by our catechisms, and the massive mankind which science tells us about – between the concrete aspirations, anxieties and responsibilities of life as expressed in a secular work and in a religious treatise . . . We need look no further than this more or less explicitly registered imbalance for the underlying source of the uneasiness which lies heavy on the mind and consciousness of so many Christians today. Contrary to the popular belief, it is not the scientific discovery of man's humble origins but much more the equally scientific

2. Christ had foretold it: 'I have yet many things to say to you, but you cannot bear them now. When the Spirit of truth comes, he will guide you into all the truth' (John 16:12-13).

discovery of a fantastic future awaiting man which is already disturbing men's hearts and should therefore prove the dominating concern of our modern apologists.

Treating it as a technical problem for the theologian, what form does it assume?

We may say that on the whole a perfectly successful way of surmounting the crisis of readjustment through which we are passing is already in sight. If scientific views on humanization are carried to their logical conclusion they assure the existence at the peak of anthropogenesis of an ultimate centre or focus of personality and consciousness, which is necessary in order to control and synthesize the genesis in history of spirit. Surely this 'Omega Point' (as I call it) is the ideal place from which to make the Christ we worship radiate – a Christ whose supernatural domination, we know, is matched by a physical power which rules the natural spheres of the world. '*In quo omnia constant*'.[3] We have here an extraordinary confluence, indeed, of what is given to us by faith and what is arrived at by reason. What used to appear to be a threat becomes a magnificent reinforcement. Far from conflicting with Christian dogma, the boundless dimensional augmentation man has just assumed in nature would thus have as its result (if carried to its ultimate conclusion) a new access of immediacy and vitality to contribute to traditional Christology.

At this point, however, we meet a basic difficulty, which contains the exact point I am commending to the earnest consideration of the professionals for whom I am writing.

Regarded *materially* in their nature as 'universal centres', the Omega Point of science and the revealed Christ coincide – as I have just said. But considered *formally*, in their mode of action, can they truly be identified with one another? On the one hand, the specific function of Omega is to cause the conscious particles of the universe to converge upon itself, in

3. 'In him all things hold together' (Col. 1:17).

order to ultra-synthesize them. On the other hand, the Christic function (in its traditional form) consists essentially in reinstating man, in restoring him, in rescuing him from an abyss. In the latter, we have a salvation through the winning of pardon; in the former, a fulfilment, through the success of an accomplished work. *In one case, a redemption; in the other, a genesis.* Are the two points of view transposable, for thought and for action? In other words, can one, *without distorting the Christian attitude,* pass from the notion of *'humanization by redemption'* to that of *'humanization by evolution'*?

Here, if I am not mistaken, is the core of the modern religious problem, and the starting point, it may well be, of a new theology.

III. A COMING THEOLOGICAL ADVANCE: THE CREATIVE ASPECT OF REDEMPTION

Before we go any further, let me first emphasize a preliminary observation.

In the history of the Church it is evident and accepted as such that dogmatic and moral views are continually being perfected by the development and inclusion of certain elements which, from appearing subordinate, gradually become essential and even preponderant. In analysis of the act of faith, the intellectual mechanism of conversion, which used to be dominated by the notion of the miraculous, is explained today chiefly by the operation of more general and less syllogistic factors, such as the wonderful coherence contributed by revelation to the whole system of our thought and action. In the area of sex, the theory of marriage, which used to centre on the duty of procreation, is now tending to place increasing emphasis on a mutual spiritual fulfilment of husband and wife. In the area of justice, the interest of moralists was formerly confined chiefly to problems of individual right; they are now concentrating, by preference, more and more on obligations that are collective and social in nature. In these various cases, and in others too, theology is evolving not by addition or subtraction of its content but by relative increase or decrease of the emphasis laid on different aspects of it – the process culminating, in fact, in the emergence each time of a concept or an attitude that is more highly synthesized.

To return now to the particular question that concerns us.

For obvious historical reasons, Christian thought and piety have hitherto given *primary* consideration in the dogma of redemption to the idea of expiatory reparation. Christ was regarded *primarily* as the Lamb bearing the sins of the world, and the world *primarily* as a fallen mass. *In addition*, however, there was from the very beginning another element in the picture – a positive element, of reconstruction or re-creation. New heavens, a new earth: these were, even for an Augustine, the fruit and the price of the sacrifice of the Cross.

Is it not conceivable – I may put it more strongly, is it not now happening – that (in line with the mechanism of the evolution of dogmas, noted above) these two elements, the positive and the negative, of the Christic influence, may be reversing their respective values, or even their natural order, in the outlook and the piety of the faithful, under the guidance of the spirit of God?

Under the pressure of today's events and the evidence we now have, the tangible world and its future developments are certainly taking on an increasing interest for the followers of the gospel. This is producing a 'humanist' revival in religion, which without in any way rejecting the dark side of creation prefers to emphasize its luminous aspect. We are even now witnessing, and taking part in, the irresistible rise of a Christian optimism.

How, then, does this optimism affect the form of our worship?

In the first place, and at a first level, Christ is tending more and more to appeal to us as leader and king of the world: this is in addition to, and as strong as, his appeal as its atoner. To purify, of course; but at the same time, to vitalize: even though the two functions are still conceived as independent, we already see them in our hearts as equipollent and conjugate.

However, this intermediate position itself already seems to have been left behind.

Put this question to the rising masses of young Christians, put it to ourselves: we are all looking and waiting, more or less consciously, for a religious efflorescence, a religious impetus – must it not come from a renewed Christology in which, however fully reparation is retained, it ceases to occupy the foreground (*in ordine naturae*) in the saving operation of the Word? *Primario*, to consummate creation in divine union; and, in order to do so, *secundario*, to annihilate the evil forces of retrogression and dispersion. No longer *first* to expiate, and then *in addition* to restore; but *first* to create (or super-create) and, in order to do so (inevitably, but incidentally), fight against evil and pay for evil. Is not that the new order in which our faith is now incontrovertibly arranging the age-old factors?

Approaching it from this angle, the transition or transformation between redemption and evolution we were looking for seems possible.

A baptism in which purification becomes a subordinate element in the total divine act of raising up the world.

A cross which symbolizes much more the ascent of creation through effort than the expiation of an offence.

A blood which circulates and vitalizes even more than it is shed.

The Lamb of God bearing, together with the sins of the world, the burden of its progress.

The idea of pardon and sacrifice enriched, and so transformed into the idea of consummation and conquest.

In other words, Christ-the-Redeemer being fulfilled, without this in any way detracting from his suffering aspect, in the dynamic plenitude of a CHRIST-THE-EVOLVER.

Such is the prospect which is without any doubt rising over our horizon.

FINAL OBSERVATION

Neither I, nor any one else, in fact, is qualified to prophesy with certainty how far tomorrow's Christianity will advance along this road which is open to us at this very moment.

One possibility, however, suggests itself to me; and this I would like to emphasize in conclusion.

For all its divine nature and immortality, the Church cannot entirely escape the universal necessity to which all organisms, no matter what their nature, are subject, the necessity of undergoing a periodic rejuvenation. After a youthful phase of expansion, every form of growth suffers a loss of tension and slackens off. This is in itself a sufficient explanation of the slowing-down the encyclicals complain of when they speak of these last centuries 'in which faith has been growing cold'. The fact is that Christianity has already been in existence for two thousand years, and the time has come (as it does for every other physical reality) when it needs to be rejuvenated by an injection of new elements.

And where are we to find the principle of this rejuvenation? There is only one source, to my mind: the fiery source, newly tapped, of 'humanization'.

For a century now, the persistently growing importance of humanity in modern thought has been a matter of concern and anxiety to defenders of religion. A new star has risen, a rival, they believed, to God; and they have constantly sought to deny its reality or diminish its brilliance.

Unless I am very much mistaken, the phenomenon has a very different significance; and very different, in consequence, must be our reaction to it.

Not only, I maintain, are human progress and the Kingdom of God not mutually contradictory – not only can these two magnetic forces fall into line with one another without interference from either side – but, what is more, there is also every likelihood that the Christian renaissance whose time is biologically due is on the point of emerging from the rightly ordered conjunction of those two forces.

That, when they are placed side by side in one and the same universe, faith in the world and faith in Christ can be reconciled with one another or even added to one another – that would already be a great point made. We can, however, gain a glimpse of and aspire to something more.

The great event with which our day is pregnant, and whose birth we must assist, may very well be, surely, that these two spiritual currents may feed, swell, and *fertilize* one another, and so, *by synthesis*, make Christianity break through into a new sphere: the very sphere in which the Redeemer, combining in himself the energies of both heaven and earth, will take his place supernaturally (as seen by our faith) at the actual focus-point upon which the rays of evolution naturally (as seen by our science) converge.

APPENDIX: ORIGINAL SIN AND EVOLUTION

To consider the possible relations between Christian salvation and human progress is basically, one must admit, to restate the vexing but unavoidable problem of the relations between original sin and evolution.

I must once more make it quite clear that I have no desire to anticipate or influence the Church's decisions on this nice point; but I do feel that it is essential to put pressure on theologians in the hope that they will concentrate their attention on two factors which they can no longer afford to overlook in their economy.

1. In the first place, and for a conglomeration of reasons which are both scientific and dogmatic, it no longer seems possible today to regard original sin as *a mere link* in the chain of historical facts. Whether we consider the organic homogeneity which science now recognizes in the physical universe, or whether we reflect on how dogma extends redemption to cosmic dimensions, we are forced, in either case, to the same conclusion. To conform to the facts of experience and at the same time to meet the demands of faith, the original Fall *cannot be located* at one given moment of time or one given place. It is not written into our past as one particular 'event'; but, transcending the limits (and taking on the general curvature) of time and space, it 'qualifies' the actual medium in which the totality of our experience develops.[4]

It appears not as *an element in a series*, but as an aspect or global modality of evolution.

2. Secondly, it is abundantly clear that the origin of evil does not raise the same difficulties (nor call for the same explanations) in a universe which is evolutive in structure, as it does in a static universe, fully formed from the outset. There is no longer any need, rationally speaking, to suspect or to look for a 'culprit'. Physical and moral disorder, of one sort or another, must necessarily be produced spontaneously in a system which is developing its organic character, *so long as* the system is incompletely organized. '*Necessarium est ut scandala*

4. 'The inevitability (as a statistical necessity, in a "population") of the appearance of sin (moral evil) at the level of man, still leaves us with the fact that it did appear, and that this appearance can be regarded as having "contaminated" the human "phylum"'; and, in consequence, that every new human being must be baptized.' Letter from Père Teilhard, 19 June 1953, in *Vues Ardentes*, p. 112 (Ed. du Seuil, Paris, 1967).

eveniant.'[5] From this point of view original sin, considered in its cosmic basis (if not in its actualization in history, among the first human beings), tends to be indistinguishable from the sheer mechanism of creation – in which it represents the action of the negative forces of 'counter-evolution'.

I would not be so bold at this point as to prophesy the repercussions this approach will undoubtedly have, sooner or later, in adding new depth and breadth of meaning to the *picture* we still form of the original offence.[6] But it is most noteworthy (and even 'elevating') that we can already say this:

'Whatever the nature of the forward step Christian thought decides to take, we may be sure that it will be in the direction of a closer organic link (closer both in co-extension and in connexion) between forces of death and forces of life inside the moving universe – and that means, ultimately, between redemption and evolution.'

Peking, 8 October 1942. Unpublished (except for the part included in *Cahier V* of the *Association des Amis de P. Teilhard de Chardin*, 'Le Christ Evoluteur', Ed. du Seuil, Paris, 1966).

5. 'It is necessary that temptations come.' The exact text of the Vulgate (Matt. 18:7) is: '*Necesse est enim ut veniant scandala.*'
  6. Conditions henceforth imposed on original sin:
    1. That it establish *the maximum Christ*.
    2. That it make possible and diffuse a maximum 'activance'. (Note by Père Teilhard.)

INTRODUCTION
TO THE CHRISTIAN LIFE
INTRODUCTION TO
CHRISTIANITY[1]

I. THE ESSENCE OF CHRISTIANITY:
'A PERSONALISTIC UNIVERSE'

From the realistic and biological point of view which is eminently that of Catholic dogma, the universe represents: (1) The arduous, personalizing unification in God of a tenuous mass of souls, distinct from God, but in subordinate dependence on him, (2) by incorporation in Christ (incarnate God), (3) through the building up of collective humano-Christian unity (Church).

'When all things are subjected to him, then the Son himself will also be subjected to him who put all things under him, that God may be everything to every one' (1 Cor. 15:28).

From this it follows that a threefold faith is necessary, and sufficient, as a foundation for the Christian position:

1. Both titles appear in Père Teilhard's manuscript, this being the second.
2. In English in the original.

1. Faith in the (personalizing) personality of God, the focus of the world.

2. Faith in the divinity of the historic Christ (not only prophet and perfect man, but also object of love and worship).

3. Faith in the reality of the Church *phylum*, in which and around which Christ continues to develop, in the world, his total personality.

Apart from these three fundamental articles, everything else in Christian teaching is basically no more than subsidiary development or explanation (historical, theological or ritual).

I shall shortly try to make it clear that although this three-fold faith is often regarded as out of date, it is in fact in line with all that is most characteristic in the views and aspirations of the modern world; but before embarking on that important question I must first note three other points, which, since they stem directly from the fundamental Christian vision, also govern the whole structure of Christian dogma. These three points are:

1. *The primacy of charity.* Since the Christian universe consists structurally in the unification of elemental persons in a supreme personality (the personality of God), the dominating and ultimate energy of the whole system can only be a person-to-person attraction: in other words, a love-attraction. God's love for the world and for each of its elements, and the elements' love, too, for one another and for God, are not, therefore, merely a secondary effect added to the creative process; they are an expression both of its operative factor and of its fundamental dynamism.

2. *The organic nature of grace.* Under the unifying influence of divine love, the spiritual elements of the world ('souls') are raised up to a higher state of life. They are 'super-humanized'. The state of union with God is accordingly much more than a mere juridical justification, associated with an extrinsic increase of divine benevolence. From the Christian, Catholic and realist

point of view, grace represents a physical super-creation. It raises us a further rung on the ladder of cosmic evolution. In other words, the stuff of which grace is made is strictly biological. This, we shall be seeing later, has a bearing on the theory of the eucharist, and, more generally, on that of all the sacraments.

3. *Infallibility of the Church.* This attribute is often misunderstood, as though it claimed to endow a particular human association with a property grotesquely out of proportion to the essentially laborious and tentative functioning of our reason. In reality, to say that the Church is infallible is simply to say that, in virtue of being a living organism, the Christian group contains in itself, and to an eminent degree, a certain sense of direction and certain potentialities: ill-defined though these are, they enable it to grope its way, constantly probing in this direction or in that, to maturity and self-fulfilment. In other words, it is simply another way of saying that the Church is a supremely living 'phylum'. That being so, to locate, as Catholics do, the permanent organ of this phyletic infallibility in the Councils – or, by an even more advanced concentration of Christian consciousness, in the Pope (formulating and expressing not his own ideas but those of the Church) – is completely in line with the great law of 'cephalization' which governs all biological evolution.

II. THE CREDIBILITY OF CHRISTIANITY:
CHRISTIANITY AND EVOLUTION

Originally, the first conversions to Christianity seem to have been largely instigated by the wonders which accompanied the preaching of the gospel. Whatever we may think of the function of the miracle in the Christian economy (see below) it is undeniable that today our reason hesitates to make its adherence to the Faith depend exclusively on the miraculous. To our minds, the criterion that finally decides on the truth of a religion can only be the capacity it shows for giving a total meaning to the universe that is being revealed to us. The 'true' religion, if it exists, must be recognized, we think, not by the brief illumination of some particular unusual event, but by a significant mark, so that under the influence and by the light of that religion, the world as a whole takes on a maximum of coherence for our intellect, and a maximum of importance for our zest for action.

From this point of view it is essential to examine, with complete objectivity, the mutual reaction upon one another at the present moment of the traditional Christian faith in Christ and the youthful modern faith in evolution. The universe, we may well believe, has now finally and permanently been appreciated by our generation as an organic whole, advancing towards an ever higher degree of freedom and personality. By that very fact, the only religion mankind wants and can henceforth acknowledge is one that is capable of justifying, assimilating and animating cosmic progress, as shown in the ascent of mankind. We have to give a categorical answer, yes or no, to the question whether Christianity has the right substance which will enable it to be *the* religion of progress for which the modern world is waiting. Its power to attract and convert our souls depends entirely on that answer.

How, then, do we stand at the present moment when it comes to the point?

There can be no denying that at first the Church watched with anxiety the development of the irresistible change in perspective which since the eighteenth century (since the Renaissance, even) has continually been replacing for us the sharply circumscribed, clearly centred and well-balanced cosmos of the ancient world, by a universe which knows no limits and is in full genesis, in space, time, and number. In our own time, however, many prejudices have been abandoned;

and the most orthodox of Christians are coming to realize three things:

1. First, when looked at from the point of view of the essential vision of the world they offer, evolution and Christianity *coincide* fundamentally. On the one hand modern evolutionism has ceased to be materialist and determinist in orientation and by definition. As the most authoritative scientists admit (Haldane, Julian Huxley, and so on) the universe, as now revealed to us by facts, is moving towards higher states of consciousness and spirituality – exactly as in the Christian *Weltanschauung*. And, on the other hand, Christianity, its sensibilities aroused by the conquests of modern thought, is finally becoming alive to the fact that its three fundamental personalist mysteries are in reality simply the three aspects of one and the same process (Christogenesis) considered either in its motive principle (creation), or in its unifying mechanism (incarnation), or in its ascensional work (redemption);[3] and so we find ourselves in the main stream of evolution.

2. Secondly, when considered in their respective expressions of evolutive personalism, evolutionism and Christianity *need one another* to support and complete each other. On the one hand (and this is too often overlooked) the Christian universal Christ would not be conceivable if the universe, which it is his function to gather to himself, did not possess (in virtue of some evolutive structure) a natural centre of convergence in which the Word could be incarnate, thence to radiate through and exert influence on the whole of the universe. On the other hand, unless some universal Christ were, positively and concretely, plain at the term of evolution, as now disclosed by human thought, that evolution would remain nebulous and uncertain, and we would not have the heart to surrender ourselves to its aspirations and demands. Evolution, we might say, preserves Christ (by making him possible), and at the same

3. See above, 'Original Sin and Redemption'. (Note by Père Teilhard.)

time Christ preserves evolution (by making it concrete and desirable).

3. Thirdly, and as a logical consequence, when evolutionism and Christianity are considered in their complementary values, all they call for is the fertilizing and *synthesizing* of one another. There are two great psychological currents which today divide the world between them – passion for the earth that has to be built up, and passion for the heaven that has to be gained. Cut off from one another these two currents run sluggish, and are the source of countless conflicts inside each one of us. By contrast, what a surge of energy there would be if Christ took his fitting and rightful place, now being restored to him (precisely in virtue of his most theological attributes), at the head of the universe in movement, and so at last the confluence were effected between the mysticism of human progress and the mysticism of charity.

The truth is that, far from running counter to modern forward-looking aspirations, the Christian faith stands as the only attitude in which a mind that is enamoured with the conquest of the world can find full and complete justification for its conviction.

Only to the Christian is it given to be able to locate at the summit of space-time not merely a vague, cold *something* but a warm and well-defined *someone*; and so *hic et nunc* only he in all the world is in a position to believe *utterly* in evolution – evolution that is no longer simply personalizing, but is personalized – and (what is psychologically even more important) to dedicate himself to it *with love*.

By its very structure Christianity is the religion made to measure for an earth that has awoken to a sense of its organic unity and its developments.

There, in short, we have the great proof of the truth of Christianity, the secret of its appeal, and the guarantee that it possesses a vitality which cannot but grow more intense as men become more conscious of their humanity.

III. THE STRONG POINTS AND THE APPARENTLY WEAK POINTS OF CHRISTIANITY: AN OVERALL VIEW

Having clarified the essence of Christianity and recognized its basic conformity with modern religious aspirations, it may be as well to consider and examine, in the light of what we have just said, a number of specially noteworthy or crucial dogmatic points – some so that they may be brought out with all the emphasis they deserve, others in order to remove certain obscurities or distortions, and in both cases in order to enable them to take their natural, functional place in the setting of a Christian 'super-evolutionism'.

1. *The Trinity*

To a modern mind, there is something over-intricate, out-landish and superfluous in the idea of a God in three persons ('Three persons in God? What's the use of that?'). And this feeling may well be exaggerated by the somewhat unenlightened way in which some of the faithful, in an attempt to keep their piety fresh, sometimes separate the Trinity from Christ in their devotion, sometimes Christ from his Father and his Spirit. In reality, if the concept of the Trinity is properly understood, it can only *strengthen* our idea of divine oneness, by giving it the *structure* (or rather the structural, built, character) which is the mark of all real living unity, in our experience. If God were not 'triune' (if, that is, he contained no inner self-distinction) we could not conceive the possibility of his sub-sisting in himself, independently, and without the reaction of some surrounding world; again, if he were not triune we could not conceive the possibility of his creating (and in consequence being incarnate) without totally immersing himself in the world he brings into being. From this point of view the trinitarian nature of God is not a concept which is without any specific relevance for our most immediate religious needs. On the contrary, it is manifestly the essential condition of God's inherent capacity to be the personal (and, in spite of the Incarnation, the transcendent) summit of a universe which is in process of personalization.

2. *The Divinity of the Historic Christ*

In the idea of a total Christ, in whom the plurality of elementary consciousnesses that make up the world develops and culminates, without absorption or loss of identity, there is nothing, as I have shown, which does not make a strong appeal to our modern way of thinking. We find it much more difficult, however, to accept that this cosmic-Christ could be localized at one moment in history in the form of a human person in space and time. As a way of overcoming, at least indirectly, this repugnance (which originates in a supposed lack of proportion between the universal-Christ and the Man-Jesus), we should bear in mind these two points:

1. In the abstract, perhaps, we can dream of a universal-Christ who could succeed in standing on his own in Christian consciousness – could lie ahead, too – without the support (without the core, we might say) of a God-man who becomes more and more lost and more and more difficult to 'check' in the growing dimness of the past; but there is no *logical* proof that such a dream conforms biologically to the structure of things. For God to be incarnate in a world in evolution means *to be born in it*; and how can he be born in it except by starting from an individual?

2. As a concrete historical fact, it is indisputable that the living and dominating idea of the universal-Christ first

appeared and developed in the consciousness of Christianity from a starting-point in the Man-Jesus recognized and worshipped as God. Even today abandonment of the historical character of Christ (that is, the divinity of the historic Christ) would mean the instant dismissal into the unreal of all the mystical energy accumulated in the Christian phylum during the last two thousand years. Christ born of the Virgin, and Christ risen from the dead: the two are one inseparable whole.

Confronted with this *factual* situation, a legitimate and 'comforting' attitude for the modern believer would appear to be to say to himself: 'Subject to every reservation about the often uncritical way in which pious writers have tried to describe the psychology of the God-man, I believe in the divinity of the Child of Bethlehem *because, in so far as,* and *in the form in which* that divinity is historically and biologically included in the reality of the universal-Christ to whom my faith and my worship are more directly attached.'

This is a confident and rational attitude, which respects and accepts all the implications of what is known for certain, and at the same time allows all the scope and freedom required for the future progress of humano-Christian thought.

3. *Revelation*

Once the personality of God has been accepted, there is no longer any difficulty in the possibility, and even the theoretical probability of a revelation, of a reflection, that is, of God on our consciousness; indeed they are seen to be eminently in line with the structure of things. In the universe, relations between elements are in all cases in proportion to the nature of those elements: they are material when between material objects, living between living beings, personal between reflective beings. Since man is personal, personal God must influence him at a personal level and in a personal form: he must influence him intellectually and affectively. In other words he must 'speak' to him. As one intellect to others, a presence cannot be dumb.

It is not quite so simple (1) to establish the historical reality of this influence and this 'word', and (2) to explain their psychological mechanism.

Those who are concerned with the theory of Christianity are still far from reaching agreement on these two points. One thing at least appears certain, that (even in the case of Christ, who *had* to make himself man to be able to speak to us) God never reveals himself to us from outside, by intrusion, but *from within*,[4] by stimulation, elevation and enrichment of the human psychic current,[5] the sound of his voice being recognizable primarily by the fullness and coherence it contributes to our individual and collective being.

This brings us to the point where we must look more closely at the doctrine of the miraculous.

4. Miracles

I have already pointed out that whereas the miracle played a dominating part in older apologetics (on the ground that it served as the divine *seal* which authenticated the teaching of the apostles and prophets), in our own days it is tending to lose some of its impact on men's minds. There are two reasons for this:

1. On the one hand, some miracles that used to be simply

4. i.e. *evolutively*. Correctly applied, this basic principle that in *all* domains (creation, redemption, revelation, sanctification) God never acts except evolutively seems to me necessary, and all that is necessary, for modernizing and giving a fresh start to Christianity. (Note by Père Teilhard.)

5. i.e. by controlled arrangement (super-arrangement) of elements (ideas and tendencies) fully pre-existing in the 'inspired author' (1947). (Note by Père Teilhard.)

accepted as such are now liable to raise serious difficulties, in as much as they might appear to be, as St Thomas would have said, not only *above* but *against* natural possibilities.

2. On the other hand, some other miracles, which used to seem a clear manifestation of a divine intervention (certain cases of healing are an example) no longer seem to us so convincing: we are beginning to suspect that organic determinisms, originating in habit and subject to the control of life, are more obedient than we thought to powers of the 'soul'.

As a result of these two acknowledged facts, the *Christian miracle* (the manifestation, that is, of a personal divine influence in Christianity) is quite naturally tending to move for us from the area of 'individual prodigies' into that of the 'general, vital success' of faith in Christ which is now in view. Today (as yesterday, no doubt, but more explicitly) the capacity shown by Christianity to hold the balance of human evolution (or anthropogenesis), to direct, animate, and fulfil it, makes us feel and recognize the hand of God in the world more certainly than does any particular extraordinary event.

Nevertheless, it remains true that Christianity would no longer be Christianity if we could not think, were it but in a vague, general way, that in every quarter, under the influence of God, cosmic determinisms and chances become more flexible, are given a final end, are breathed into, in step with our union with God and our prayer. Yet, whatever inner evidence we may have on this matter (and such evidence is perhaps much more certain than any reasoning), we cannot but recognize that the objectivity of such special or general interventions by Providence into our lives falls into the category of personal intuition rather than into that of the demonstrable.

Finally, and this is something we can never get away from, we cannot recognize God's hand and voice in the world without a special sensitizing of the eyes and ears and of our soul ('grace') – that is, without a special sort of sense or super-sense, whose existence, we should note (if union with God does indeed correspond to a higher degree of life), is perfectly in harmony with the laws of biology.

N.B. In a certain number of cases (the virginity of Mary, Christ's material resurrection, the Ascension, and so on) we get the impression that the gospel miracles express in concrete form (like Genesis) the 'unrepresentable' element in events as profound as the absorption of the Word into the human phylum, or Christ's transition from his individual state to his 'cosmic' state as centre of evolution. This is not simply a matter of symbols: rather is it the expression in image of something which is inexpressible. From this it follows that it would be as idle to subject such images to a scientific criticism (since they correspond to nothing patient of photographic representation) as it would be disastrous to reject them (since this would be to rob Christogenesis of its trans-experiential essence).

5. Original Sin and Redemption

The Christian's sign is the Cross; and the first meaning of the Cross is the expiation of an 'original offence', as a result of which mankind, we are told, suddenly fell into a state of sin, suffering and death.

For a modern mind there is nothing initially more difficult to accept than this representation of the Fall: not only would it appear to be contradicted by a palaeontology and a prehistory which can find no place either for the primitive conception of the earthly paradise or for an originally perfected human couple – it conflicts, too, with an informed optimism which has come to regard human evolution as being effected along a continuous trajectory. Nothing is more difficult to accept; and yet there is nothing, fortunately, which more clearly illuminates the power of renewal and adaptation proper to the Christian phylum.

Take the idea of 'salvation': simply in virtue of the co-existence and vital confrontation of faith in the Redemption and faith in evolution, what form is it now coming naturally to assume deep down in the souls of the faithful?

On the one hand, if the original transgression is transposed to the dimensions of the universe, as we now see it in the organic whole of time and space, it tends more and more to link up (at least in its roots) with the law of ever-possible fall and ever-present suffering in a world which is in a state of evolution. On the other hand, the Christian mind, without losing sight of the 'expiatory' aspect of Christ's saving operation, is much more inclined than heretofore to concentrate its attention on the aspect of 'recasting and building'.

On both grounds I believe that I am right in saying that a spiritual transformation is going on, slowly but surely, at the end of which the suffering Christ, without ceasing to be 'he who bears the sins of the world', indeed precisely as such, will become more and more in the eyes of believers 'he who bears and supports the weight of the world in evolution'.

Under our very eyes, and in our hearts, I am convinced, Christ-the-Redeemer is fulfilling himself and unfolding himself in the figure of Christ-the-Evolver. Thereby, too, the meaning of the Cross is taking on greater breadth and dynamism for us: the Cross which is now the symbol not merely of the dark retrogressive side of the universe in genesis, but also and, even more, of its triumphant and luminous side; the Cross which is the symbol of progress and victory won through mistakes, disappointments and hard work; the only Cross, in very truth, that we can honestly, proudly and passionately offer for the worship of a world that has become conscious of what it was yesterday and what awaits it tomorrow.

6. Hell

The existence of a hell is, in company with the mystery of the Cross, one of the most alarming and most criticized aspects of the Christian Creed. Yet, when this dogma is reduced to its essence, nothing is more in harmony with the outlook of a universe in evolution. Every evolution (so far as our experience goes) involves selection and rejection. If, therefore, we look at the whole of the process of the world's unification in God, it is impossible for us to conceive it without allowing (logically, if not factually) for what might possibly find a way of escaping this beatifying process. Can the operation of saving man, in which creation consists, give a hundred-per-cent result? Christianity does not give an unqualified yes or no; but it reminds us that there can be loss – and that in that case the 'reprobate' elements would be eliminated for ever, that is, they would be exiled to the opposite pole from God.

From this point of view, to assert the existence of hell is simply a negative way of saying that, by physical and organic necessity, man can attain his happiness and fulfilment only by being true to the movement which carries him along, and so reaching the term of his evolution. Supreme life (that is, a full consciousness of all in all), or supreme death (that is, a consciousness infinitely disunited in itself). All or nothing. That is the alternative presented to us by existence and expressed in the idea of hell. Would anyone be so rash as to say that such a condition is not in complete conformity with what we know and with all that we can reasonably anticipate; or, even more, that it is not a tribute to the importance of life and of human dignity?

If we accept that, there is no need to go further and allow ourselves to be drawn into misleading attempts to *represent* or form an *imaginary picture* of hell. Hell, it cannot be said too often, is known to us and has meaning only in so far as it occupies in our outlook the opposite place from heaven, as being the opposite pole from God. This means that we can define it only negatively, in relation to the heaven which it is not. Every attempt to objectify it and describe it in itself as an isolated whole may well lead us (as we know only too well) into producing a ridiculous and repulsive picture.

In short, hell is an 'indirect' reality which we cannot help feeling intensely, but without it being either profitable or possible for us to perceive it and take a straight look at it – we are like the mountaineer who is all the time aware of the colossal drop behind him, while the essence of his tactics and the success of his climb depends on keeping his back turned to it.

I would not go so far as to say that the views put forward here are as yet generally accepted by the theoreticians of the Christian faith; but they are even so gaining ground among believers and becoming established as a practical answer. There is every likelihood, accordingly, that they will express the living orthodoxy of tomorrow.

7. *The Eucharist*

From the realistic point of view which is universally characteristic of Catholic Christianity, the sacraments are more than a symbolic rite. What they stand for, they effect biologically in the domain of the life of personal union with God. Nowhere does this idea of the organic function of the sacrament stand out more clearly than in the eucharist (mass and communion).

To read the catechisms, one might imagine that all the sacraments were equally important, and that the eucharist was one of a number of sacraments, just like the others. In reality the eucharist belongs to an order of its own among the sacraments. It is the first of the sacraments, or rather it is the one sacrament to which all the others are related; and this for the good reason that the *axis* of the Incarnation, that is to say of creation, runs directly through the eucharist.

Consider, still from the Catholic-Christian point of view, what happens when we go to communion.

In the first place, and immediately, we enter personally into physiological contact, at the moment of communion, with the assimilative power of the incarnate Word. What is more, however, this particular contact – our *nth* communion, say – does not follow on discontinuously from the *n* communions which preceded it in our life; it combines organically with the earlier communions in the unity of a single spiritual development, co-extensive with the whole duration of our life. All the communions of our life are, in fact, only successive instants or episodes in one single communion – in one and the same process of Christification.

Even this is not the whole story.

What is true of me is true of every other Christian, living, dead, or still to be born; further, both reason and faith tell us that all these Christians make up, in mankind and in God, but one whole, organically linked in a common super-life. If, then, all my own communions form but one single great communion, then all the communions of all men of all times, taken as one great whole, also add up to but one single and even vaster communion, co-extensive in this case with the history of mankind. This amounts to saying that when the eucharist is considered in the complete effecting of its operation, it is simply the expression and the manifestation of God's unifying energy applied individually to each spiritual atom of the universe.

To put it briefly, to adhere to Christ in the eucharist is inevitably and *ipso facto* to incorporate ourselves a little more fully on each occasion in a Christogenesis, which itself (and it is in this, as we have seen, that the essence of Christian faith consists) is none other than the soul of universal cosmogenesis.

For the Christian who has understood this profound economy, and who at the same time is fully alive to the organic unity of the universe, to receive communion is not, accordingly, a sporadic, localized, particulate act. When such a Christian communicates with the Host, he realizes that he is in contact with the very heart of evolution. And, vice versa, he sees that if he is to come into contact with the heart of the Host, he must necessarily communicate, by acceptance and fulfilment of his whole life, with the whole surface, the whole depth, the whole body of the world in evolution.

The eucharist is the sacrament of our life, experienced and mastered, in its individual modalities as well as in its cosmic extension: 'super-communion'!

8. *Catholicism and Christianity*

Catholics are often reproached by other Christians for seeking to monopolize Christ for themselves – as though there were no true religion outside Catholicism. After what has been said earlier about the living and evolutive nature of the Christian faith it is easy to understand that this privilege claimed by the Church of Rome of being the only authentic expression of Christianity is not an unjustified pretension but meets an inevitable organic need.

There is a fact which we noted in a general way at the beginning; and our analysis of a number of dogmatic points, still today in full process of 'evolution', has allowed us to confirm it historically in detail: in virtue of its essence, Christianity is much more than a fixed system, presented to us once and for all, of truths which have to be accepted and preserved literally. For all its resting on a core of 'revelation', it represents in fact a spiritual attitude which is continually developing; it is the development of a Christic consciousness in step with, and to meet the needs of, the growing consciousness of mankind. Biologically, it behaves as a 'phylum'; and by biological necessity it must, therefore, have the structure of a phylum; in other words, it must form a coherent and progressive system of collectively associated spiritual elements.

That being so, it is evident that *hic et nunc* there is nothing within Christianity except Catholicism which possesses such characteristics.

There are, no doubt, many individuals outside Catholicism who recognize and love Christ, and are therefore united to him, as much as (and even more than) some Catholics. But these individuals are not grouped together in the 'cephalized' unity of a *body* which reacts vitally, as an organic whole, to the combined forces of Christ and mankind. They benefit from the sap in the trunk without sharing in its early development and youthful surge at the heart of the tree. Experience proves this: as a matter not only of logic but of fact, it is only in Catholicism that new dogmas continue to germinate – and, in a more general way, it is only in Catholicism that the new attitudes are developed which, by continually synthesizing the old Creed and views that have newly emerged into human consciousness, pave the way in our world for the coming of Christian humanism.

Everything goes to show that if Christianity is in truth destined to be, as it professes, and as it is conscious of being, the religion of tomorrow, it is only through the living, organic axis of its Roman Catholicism that it can hope to measure up to the great modern humanist currents and become one with them.

To be Catholic is the only way of being fully and utterly Christian.

9. *Christian Holiness*

All the great religions set out to raise man above matter, which means to spiritualize him, which again means to 'sanctify' him.

Yet the definition of 'saint' or holy varies from one religion to another, as do the notions also of spirit and matter. What is the Christian position on this essential point?

In principle, and in a general way, we may say that the original characteristic of Christian ascesis has been from the outset a concern to respect the integrity, body and soul, of the 'human compound'. In the majority of Eastern religions matter, being regarded as evil, had to be gradually left behind in the course of sanctification; Christianity, on the other hand, maintains the value and rights of the flesh, which the Word assumed, and which he is going to raise to life again. At the same time as Christ saves spirit, he saves matter in which he immersed himself. Similarly, the Christian does not have to try to annihilate his body but to sanctify and sublimate it.

When we come to examine exactly what this sublimation consists in, we find that the Church's attitude is again in line with her living, progressive nature; she appears to be clarifying her views in an ascetical and mystical evolution which is closely linked with the elucidation of her dogmatic thought. Until quite recently (so long, that is, as matter and spirit could still be regarded as two heterogeneous elements statically coupled together in the world) the Christian saint was the man who was the most successful in introducing order into this dualist complex, by reducing physical energies to the position of being subservient to the aspirations of the spirit. Once again, as in the Eastern religions, this resulted in a predominant emphasis on mortification.

A different view now prevails: in a universe whose evolutive structure has finally been appreciated, matter and spirit are now seen as two terms mutually integrated in the unity of one and the same movement (spirit emerging experientially in the world only upon progressively more fully synthesized matter). In consequence of this, the question of ascesis assumes a different form. For the Christian of today it is no longer sufficient to introduce the reign of peace and silence into his body, so that his soul may be free to devote itself to the things of God. What matters to him, if he is to attain perfection, is above all to extract from his body all the *spiritual power* it contains – and not merely from this body strictly confined to its limbs of flesh, but from the whole immense 'cosmic' body which is made up for each of us by the enveloping mass of the *Weltstoff* in evolution.

As we now see things, with everything becoming sacred because capable of spiritualization, the gospel's 'Leave all and follow me' can ultimately only mean that it sends us back to 'all' seen in a higher perspective, in as much as this 'all' (we now realize) enables us to take hold of Christ and further his being in the universality of his incarnation. The emphasis now is not primarily on mortification – but on the perfecting of man's effort through mortification.

The saint, the Christian saint, as we now understand him and look for him, will not be the man who is the most successful in escaping from matter and mastering it completely; he will be the man who seeks to make all his powers – gold, love, or freedom – transcend themselves and co-operate in the consummation of Christ, and who so realizes for us the ideal of the faithful servant of evolution.[6]

---

6. Since the mystical way followed by Père Teilhard – the '*Via Tertia*', as he called it – has given rise to erroneous interpretations, it is important to emphasize the distinction he drew, until the end of his life, between 'mastering matter completely' and 'making it transcend itself'. It was in this 'sublimation', which rules out personal enjoyment, that as a religious he followed unswervingly the road he chose when he made his vows: 'To hallow, through chastity, poverty and obedience, the power enclosed in love, in gold, in independence' ('The Priest', in *Writings in Time of War*, Collins, London, and Harper & Row, New York, 1968, p. 222).

CONCLUSION: CHRISTIANITY AND PANTHEISM

The whole of the foregoing exposition makes it clear that Christianity is pre-eminently a faith in the progressive unification of the world in God; it is essentially universalist, organic and 'monist'.

There is obviously some special quality in this 'pan-Christic' monism. Since, from the Christian point of view, the universe is finally and permanently unified only through personal relations (that is, under the influence of *love*) the unification of beings in God cannot be conceived as being effected by fusion, with God being born from the welding together of the elements of the world, or on the contrary by absorbing them in himself. It must be effected by 'differentiating' synthesis, with the elements of the world becoming more themselves, the more they converge on God. For it is the specific effect of love to accentuate the individuality of the beings it associates more closely. Ultimately, God is not alone in the totalized Christian universe (in the pleroma, to use St Paul's word); but he is all in all of us ('*en pasi panta theos*'): unity in plurality.

This, we should always remember, is not a restriction or an attenuation: it is a perfection and an accentuation of the idea of unity. It is *only* in fact the 'pantheism' of love or Christian 'pantheism' (that in which each being is super-personalized, super-centred, by union with Christ, the divine super-centre) – it is only that pantheism which correctly interprets and fully satisfies the religious aspirations of man, whose dream is ultimately to lose self consciously in unity. That pantheism alone agrees with experience, which shows us that in every instance *union differentiates*. And finally, it alone legitimately continues the curve of evolution, on which the centration of the universe upon itself advances only through organic complexity.

Contrary to an over-popular preconception, it is in Christianity (provided it is understood in the fullness of its Catholic realism) that the pantheist mysticism of all times, and more particularly of our own day (when it is so dominated by 'creative evolutionism') can reach its highest, most coherent and most dynamic form, the form that is most instinct with worship.

And that is why, I say once more, Christianity has every chance of being the one true religion of tomorrow.

Unpublished, Peking, 29 June 1944.

CHRISTIANITY AND EVOLUTION: SUGGESTIONS FOR A NEW THEOLOGY

FOREWORD

IN the course of the last twenty years I have put forward in a long series of essays the views which gradually took shape in my mind on the emergence in the thought of modern man of a Christian evolutionism. Unfortunately, or fortunately, many of these pieces have never been published. Moreover it generally happened that every one of them contained only provisional or incompletely worked out observations on this subject. Now that my ideas have matured – and in so far as they may be a useful contribution to the Christian effort – it seems to me worth while at last to offer them, in their essence, as a coherent whole: reduced, that is, to the form of a small number of organically linked basic propositions. This schematic presentation will be handier and should bring out more clearly whatever may be fruitful in my thought or, on the other hand, may be open to criticism. Anything vital in it will have a chance of surviving and adding something to itself; and then my work will be done.

As the title of this essay indicates, I am writing only in the hope of making a personal contribution to the work which is common to the Christian consciousness: an expression of the demands made, in my own particular case, by '*fides quaerens intellectum*'.[1] These are suggestions, not affirmation or teaching. For reasons that derive from the very structure of my outlook, I am deeply convinced that religious thought cannot develop

1. 'Faith seeking understanding.'

except traditionally, collectively, and 'phyletically'. In what I am saying here, accordingly, my only wish and my only hope is to *'sentire'* – or rather *'praesentire'* – *cum Ecclesia*.[2]

A. THE PRESENT RELIGIOUS SITUATION: FAITH IN GOD AND FAITH IN THE WORLD: A NECESSARY SYNTHESIS

1. It is a commonplace that, religiously speaking, the world is growing cold. In reality it has never been more aglow with heat. But it is a new fire, as yet imperfectly distinguished and identified, which is beginning to take hold of the earth. Under the influence of a large number of convergent causes (the discovery of organic time and space, progress in the unification or 'planetization' of man, etc.), man has quite certainly become alive, for the last century, to the evidence that he is involved in a vast process of anthropogenesis, cosmic in plane and dimensions. The direct result of this awakening has been to stimulate, from the youthful 'magmatic' depths of his being, a surge (as yet amorphous, but powerful) of limitless aspirations and hopes. Whether it be the roar of the waves of social upheavals, or the clamour of the Press and the flood of new books, to an informed or practised ear the clatter of discord now rising from the human mass echoes one single fundamental note – faith and hope in some salvation associated with the evolutionary fulfilment of the earth. No, the modern world is not irreligious – far from it. It is simply that the sudden injection of a massive dose of a new life-sap is making the *religious spirit*, in its very stuff and in one mass, boil up and take on a new form.

2. Deep-seated troubles must inevitably make themselves felt within Christianity as a direct result of this 'eruption'. Christian dogmatics, formulated and adapted to meet the dimensions of an earlier (antecedent) state of human religious energy, is

2. 'To share or anticipate the feeling of the Church.'

no longer functioning in a way that correctly meets the requirements of an *'anima naturaliter Christiana'*,[3] Mark 2. This is obviously at the root of our generation's characteristic indifference to the Church's teachings. As Nietzsche pointed out, it is not that the gospel arguments have lost their force – the gospel itself has lost its appeal, irresistibly overlaid by a higher appeal; and this (in spite of their desperate attempts to retain it) is true even of a surprising number of religious and priests. And yet is not Christianity today the *only* human current in sight in which faith (essential for the future of all anthropogenesis) in a personal and personalizing centre of the universe is alive and has some chance of surviving?

3. Seen from this angle, the psychological situation of the world today is as follows: On one side there is an innate, tumultuous upsurge of cosmic and humanist aspirations; they emerge from the unsounded depths of human consciousness; they are irresistible in their rise but dangerously ill-defined, and, what is even more dangerous, they are still 'impersonal' in their expression. That upsurge is the new faith in the world. And on the other side there are the vision and the anticipation of a transcendent and loving pole of the universe; it is unswervingly upheld by Christian dogma but, to all appearances, more and more abandoned by the main stream of religion; and this is the ancient faith in God. As for the meaning of this conflict and as for deciding how it is going to develop, that problem, to my mind, is solved by the very way in which we have just presented it. Surely the two terms – faith in the world and faith in God – so far from being antagonistic, are structurally complementary? On one side, represented by modern humanism, we have a sort of neo-paganism, bursting with life, but still 'acephalous' – headless. On the other, in the form of Christianity, we have a head in which the blood no longer circulates at the necessary speed. On one, the fantastic-

3. 'Naturally Christian soul.'

ally enlarged stratified surfaces of a cone which are nevertheless incapable of closing up on themselves: a cone that has no apex. On the other, an apex which has lost its base: two detached parts, it is plain, that clamour to be joined together.

4. To put it briefly, Christianity has now enjoyed two thousand years of existence; it must obey an organic rhythm to which everything in nature would appear to be subject, and, precisely because it is immortal, the time has come when it cannot continue to exist without being rejuvenated and re-fashioned – and not by a change in its structure but by the assimilation of new elements. In other words what we must recognize in this present crisis, in which we can see and feel the confrontation between the traditional Christian forces and the modern forces of evolution, is simply the permutations of a providential and indispensable inter-fertilization. I am sure that this is so; but in that case it is clear that if the synthesis is to be effected Christianity must, without modifying the position of its peak, open up its axes to include in its totality the new surge of religious energy which is rising from below in its effort to be sublimated.

We must consider, then, how it may be possible, in the dual domain of theology and mysticism, for the guiding principles of Christianity to be expanded, without being distorted, to the dimensions of a universe which has been fantastically enlarged and integrated by modern scientific thought.

B. A NEW THEOLOGICAL ORIENTATION: THE UNIVERSAL CHRIST

5. We may say, in a general way, that the predominant concern of theology in the first centuries of the Church was to determine, intellectually and mystically, Christ's relation to the Trinity. In our own time the vitally important question has become for it to analyse and define the links between Christ

and the universe: how they stand in relation to one another, and how they influence one another.

6. So far as the nature of the universe is concerned, it is becoming more and more evident that the fundamental problem the modern age presents to the Christian philosopher is that of *the specific value of* 'participated being'. Classical ontology is logically obliged to define the created world as completely contingent, the object of pure mercy: as such, whether we look at it from the point of view of modern man, or from the Christian point of view, the world is in both cases found to be *unsatisfying*. From the human point of view, a doctrine which *no longer justifies* the vastness nor the arduousness of the evolution in which we can *see* we are involved, is a brutal contradiction, we feel, of what is intellectually apparent to us; but, what is more, it undermines the very driving impulse of our action. What does 'being beatified' matter if, when all is said and done, our lives make no 'absolute' contribution to the totality of being? And at the same time, from the Christian point of view, we can no longer understand why, by pure 'benevolence', a God could commit himself to releasing so much suffering and placing so many hazards in our path. You may drive our reason into a corner as remorselessly as you please, by a dialectic of pure act; but you will never convince our hearts that the vast enterprise of the cosmos, *as now revealed to us*, is no more than a gift or a divine plaything. And further, if that were so, why the supreme importance attached by the most fully attested scriptural texts to the completion of the mysterious pleroma? God is entirely self-sufficient; and yet the universe contributes *something that is vitally necessary to him*: those are the two apparently contradictory conditions which participated being must in future satisfy *explicitly*, if it is to fulfil its twofold function of 'activating' our will and 'pleromizing' God. Old as religious thought itself, but given new youth and life by the discovery of evolution, the

antinomy still seems as insoluble as ever. In order to solve it, should we not take a lesson from physics, which had no hesitation in changing its geometry when the pressure of facts demanded it? Should we not, then, simply decide at last to create a higher metaphysics which includes a further dimension?

Supposing, for example, we replace a metaphysics of *Esse* by a metaphysics of *Unire* – which comes to much the same thing as once again imitating physics in the substitution, forced upon it by experience, of motion for the mobile in phenomena. What happens? In the metaphysics of *Esse*, pure act, once posited, monopolizes all that is absolute and necessary in being; and, no matter what one does, nothing can then justify the existence of participated being. In a metaphysics of union, on the other hand, we can see that, when once immanent divine unity is complete, a degree of absolute *unification* is still possible: that which would restore to the divine centre an 'antipodial' aureole of pure multiplicity. Defined as being in tension towards a final state of maximum unification, the universal system contains an additional 'freedom'. The created, which is 'useless', superfluous, on the plane of being, becomes essential on the plane of union. Surely this is a profitable line to explore?[4]

6 (ii). Whatever solution is adopted, the organic vastness of the universe obliges us to rethink the notion of divine *omni-sufficiency*: God fulfils himself, he in some way completes himself, in the pleroma. Still from the same angle of approach, we have to make a further readjustment in our thought as it

4. From this point of view, we might say that for the discursive reason *two phases* can be distinguished in 'theogenesis'. In the first, God posits himself in his trinitarian structure ('fontal' being reflecting itself, self-sufficient, upon itself): 'Trinization'. In the second phase, he envelops himself in participated being, by evolutive unification of pure multiple ('positive non-being') born (in a state of absolute potency) by antithesis to pre-posited trinitarian unity: *Creation*. (Note by Père Teilhard.)

affects the idea of *omnipotence*. In the earlier conception, God could create, (1) instantaneously, (2) isolated beings, (3) as often as he pleased. We are now beginning to see that creation can have only one object: *a universe*; that (observed *ab intra*) creation can be effected only by an *evolutive process* (of personalizing synthesis); and that it can come into action *only once*: when 'absolute' multiple (which is produced by antithesis to trinitarian unity) is reduced, nothing is left to be united either in God or 'outside' God.

The recognition that 'God cannot create except evolutively' provides a radical solution for our reason to the problem of evil (which is a direct 'effect' of evolution), and at the same time explains the manifest and mysterious association of matter and spirit.

7. In the matter of Christ's relation to the world, the whole present theological problem would appear to centre on the rise in Christian consciousness of what we might call the *Universal-Christ*. This is a point of capital importance, which must be fully understood.

Hitherto, the thought of the faithful could hardly be said explicitly to distinguish in practice more than two aspects of Christ: the Man-Jesus and the Word-God. Yet it is clear that a third aspect of the theandric complex was left in the background. By that I mean the mysterious super-human person constantly underlying the Church's most fundamental institutions and most solemn dogmatic affirmations: He in whom all was created – he *'in quo omnia constant'*[5] – he who, by his birth and his blood, restores every creature to his Father; the Christ of the eucharist and the parousia, the cosmic, consummating Christ of St Paul. Until today, I repeat, this third aspect of the *incarnate* Word has been insufficiently distinguished from the other two – for lack, apparently, of a concrete, 'phenomenal' substratum which could be materialized in Christian thought

5. 'In whom all things hold together' (Col. 1:17).

and piety. But consider what is happening today. Under the combined influence of men's thoughts and aspirations, the universe around us is seen to be knit together and convulsed by a vast movement of convergence. Not only theoretically, but experientially, our modern cosmogony is taking the form of a cosmogenesis (or rather a psycho- or noo-genesis) at the term of which we can distinguish a supreme focus of personalizing personality. Who can fail to see the support, the reinforcement, the stimulus which this discovery of the physical pole of universal synthesis contributes to our view of revelation? Just suppose that we *identify* (at least in his 'natural' aspect) the cosmic Christ of faith with the Omega Point of science: then everything in our outlook is clarified and broadened, and falls into harmony. First, the term of the world's physico-biological evolution no longer appears indeterminate to our reason: it has been given a concrete peak, a heart, a face. And secondly there is the effect on our faith. The exaggerated properties attributed to the incarnate Word by tradition lose their metaphysical and juridical character; they take their place smoothly and realistically among and at the head of the most fundamental of the currents now recognized in the universe by science. Christ's is indeed, we must admit, a fantastic position; but, just because it is fantastic, it fits the true scale of things. The fact is, that the keystone of the arch to be built is there in our own hands. If we are to effect the synthesis between faith in God and faith in the world, for which our generation is waiting, there is nothing better we can do than dogmatically to bring out, in the person of Christ, the cosmic aspect and function which make him organically the prime mover and controller, the 'soul', of evolution.

In the first century of the Church, Christianity made its definitive entry into human thought by boldly identifying the Christ of the gospel with the Alexandrian Logos. The logical continuation of the same tactics and the prelude to the same success must be found in the instinct which is now urging the faithful, after two thousand years, to return to the same policy; but this time it must not be with the ordinating principle of the stable Greek kosmos but with the neo-Logos of modern philosophy – the evolutive principle of a universe in movement.

8. Objections have, I know, been raised to this generalization of Christ-the-Redeemer in a true 'Christ-the-Evolver' (he who, with the sins, bears the whole weight of the world in progress); to this elevation of the historic Christ to a universal physical function; to this final identification of cosmogenesis with a Christogenesis. It has been said that all this may well mean that the human reality of Jesus Christ is lost in the super-human and vanishes in the cosmic. Nothing, I believe, is more baseless than such doubts. The more, indeed, we think about the profound laws of evolution, the more convinced we must be that the universal Christ could not appear at the end of time at the peak of the world, if he had not previously entered it during its development, *through the medium of birth*, in the form of an *element*. If it is indeed true that it is through Christ-Omega that the universe in movement holds together, then, correspondingly, it is from his concrete germ, the Man of Nazareth, that Christ-Omega (both theoretically and historically) derives his whole consistence, as a hard experiential fact. The two terms are intrinsically one whole, and they cannot vary, in a truly total Christ, except simultaneously.

9. So far, we have concentrated our attention on the new relationships emerging between the incarnate Word and a universe which is henceforth conceived as unitary and evolutive in nature. It is obvious, however, that every theological development which affects the theology of the 'Son-Object-of-Love' must have repercussions on the theology of the Father, in whom all being must ultimately find its source. Would it be unfair to say of the divine Fatherhood, the first and fundamental gospel message, that this mystery has hitherto been

thought of by Christians at a level that is still 'neolithic', that is to say in its most juridical, 'familial' aspect? The Father: he who rules, fosters, pardons, rewards . . . But why not go further and say 'he who vitalizes and engenders'? There is a point here which needs to be watched: a change of spiritual value has a way of creeping into words as there is a modification of the underlying thought in the background. The 'paterfamilias', the King – today these symbols have lost their magic for us. In future our age can only worship something more penetrating, more organic, vaster, something that rises above every human value. Without in any way detracting from the personal warmth of the divine centre, we have to present it as radiating ever more powerfully from the seminal, eternal, stream of the creative act. We have to see its brilliance at the triune focus of Omega Point. Only then shall we be able once again to say, from hearts that have been completely won over and convinced, 'Our Father which art in heaven'.

10. Creation, Incarnation, Redemption. Until today these three fundamental mysteries of the Christian faith, while indissolubly linked *in fact* in the history of the world, have remained *logically* independent of one another. God could, it appeared, dispense with the universe, subject to no restriction of any sort. He could create without making himself incarnate. The Incarnation, in turn, could have involved neither labour nor suffering. If these same three mysteries are transposed from the old cosmos (static, limited, and open at every moment to rearrangement) into the modern universe (organically welded by its space-time into a single evolutive whole), they tend to form but one mystery. In the first place, without creation, something, it would appear, would be absolutely lacking to God, considered in the fullness not of his being but of his act of union (cf. 5. above). By definition, then, to create is for God to unite himself to his work, that is to say in one way or another to involve himself in the world by incarnation. And is

not 'to be incarnate' *ipso facto* to share in the sufferings and evils inherent in the painfully concentrating multiple? Creation, Incarnation, Redemption: seen in this light, the three mysteries become in reality no more, for the new Christology, than the three aspects of one and the same fundamental process: they are aspects of a *fourth* mystery, which alone, when finally examined by thought, is absolutely justifiable and valid. To distinguish this mystery from the other three we must have a name for it: it is the mystery of the creative union of the world in God, or Pleromization.[6] Is there anything in what I have said that is not both extremely Christian and extremely consistent? In classical theology, we might say, dogma used to be presented to our reason as a series of independent circles distributed over a plane. Today, reinforced by a new dimension (that of the universal-Christ) the same pattern is tending to develop and come together organically on one and the same sphere inside space: the effect, marvellous in its simplicity, of *hyper-orthodoxy*.

C. A NEW MYSTICAL ORIENTATION: THE LOVE OF EVOLUTION

11. Reduced to the initial and still crude form in which it is now emerging in the modern world, the new religious spirit appears, as we have said (cf. 1), as the impassioned vision and anticipation of some super-mankind. This super-mankind (the highest term the cosmic effort can attain in the prospect open to us) still presents itself to us only in the extremely ill-defined guise of an impersonal collective. As yet, therefore, the movement towards worship which it stimulates in human consciousness can be expressed, *at this stage*, only in terms of rational

6. 'The pleroma *is more* (in absolute value) than "God alone" before Christ has entered into it "with the world incorporated in himself". The pleromization of being must one day be linked to "trinitization in some generalized ontology"' (Letter to Père J. M. Le Blond, April 1953).

intelligence and will: recognition of the existence of the movement which is totalizing us, and adaptation to it. In this use of
our faculties, there is still no satisfaction for the heart, with all
that that word implies of vital and dynamic fullness. Supposing,
on the other hand (as demanded by the theological synthesis
explained in 5), the universal-Christ assumes the place and
fulfils the function of Omega Point: we shall then find that
a warm light spreads from top to bottom and over the whole
cross-section of the cosmic layers, rising up from the nethermost
depths of things. With cosmogenesis being transformed, as we
said, into Christogenesis, it is the stuff, the main stream, the
very being of the world which is now *being personalized.*
Someone, and no longer something, is in gestation in the
universe. To believe and to serve was not enough: we now
find that it is becoming not only possible but *imperative* literally
to *love* evolution.

12. Analysed from the Christian point of view, as spontaneously and necessarily born from contact between faith in
Christ and faith in the world, love of evolution is not a mere
extension of love of God to one further object. It corresponds
to a radical reinterpretation (one might almost say it emerges
from a recasting) of the notion of charity. 'Thou shalt love
God.' 'Thou shalt love thy neighbour for the love of God.'
In its new form, 'Thou shalt love God in and through the
genesis of the universe and of mankind', this twofold gospel
commandment is synthesized into a single meaningful act,
with an as yet unparalleled field of application and power to
make new. Indeed, as a result of this simple transposition (still
only made *possible* today by a decisive advance in human reflection) Christian charity is forthwith both dynamized, universalized and (if I may be allowed the word, taken in its most
legitimate meaning) 'pantheized'.

a. *Dynamized:* no longer merely to ease the suffering, to
bind up the wounds, to succour the weakness, of mankind;

but, through every form of effort and discovery, to urge its powers, by love, right up to their higher term.

b. *Universalized:* no longer merely to concentrate our attention and our concern on souls adrift in a neutral or hostile universe; but, with passionate drive, to accept and urge on the complete and total operation of the cosmic forces in which the universal-Christ is born and fulfilled in each one of us.

c. *'Pantheized':* no longer to adhere vitally to God through some central and specially favoured point of our being; but to communicate, to 'super-communicate', with him (without fusion or confusion – for as love unites its terms, so it differentiates and personalizes them) through all the height, the breadth, the depths and the multiplicity of the organic powers of space and time.

13. Contemporary humanism reproaches the gospel attitude, not without reason, for proving inapplicable to the scale of the modern world and impracticable. How could the world, as we are coming to see it today, possibly be built with the spirit of non-resistance to evil and of detachment from earthly things preached by the letter of the Sermon on the Mount? Christianity has been accused of bankruptcy or surrender. These contradictions vanish in the blaze of super-charity radiated by the universal-Christ. Love God in and through the universe in evolution: we can imagine no more constructive rule of action, none more all-embracing, none with more appeal, more exactly fitted to every case, and yet none more open to all the unpredictable demands of the future. It is indeed, as I say, a theological rule of action. But even more it is an *actually living* neo-mysticism in which an irresistible urge to combine under the sign of Christianity is felt in every modern conscious mind by the two fundamental attractions that have hitherto so woefully divided man's power to worship between heaven and earth, between theocentricism and anthropocentricism.

14. Looked at from a general psychological point of view,

this new attitude is historically the most complex and the most unified state human consciousness has yet attained. We can see no other direction in which it could continue and centre itself at a still higher level. Indeed, in the 'act of super-charity' all possible forms of intellection and volition can be foreseen as indefinitely capable of sublimation, of synthesis, and (if I may use the word) of being 'amorized'. Love, in consequence, is undoubtedly the single higher form towards which, as they are transformed, all the other sorts of spiritual energy converge – as one might expect in a universe built on the plane of union and by the forces of union.

Nevertheless we must never forget that this great phenomenon is intrinsically dependent on the development of the universal-Christ in our souls. That is why, the more we observe the present great movements of human thought, the more convinced we feel that it is around Christianity (considered in its 'phyletic', that is to say its Catholic, form) that the main axis of hominization is becoming ever more closely defined.

Unpublished, Peking, 11 November 1945.

REFLECTIONS ON
ORIGINAL SIN[1]

I. INTRODUCTION

IN the course of a few generations there have been a number of important and interconnected changes in our view of the world; they have been brought about much less by the introduction of new material objects than by the appearance (by which I mean the perception) of certain new *dimensions* in the field of our experience. First among these we may instance:

a. the temporo-spatial *organicity* of the universe, in virtue of which every element and every event (however limited their apparent trajectory in history) are in reality – by what leads up to them, by their present condition, and by what they will develop into – co-extensive with the whole of a limitless space-time;[2]

b. the *atomicity* of the stuff of the cosmos: this is a characteristic the Greeks had already had more than a hint of, but it is only some few years since it was scientifically established in its full realism and its almost terrifying degree. In virtue of this atomicity the self-organization of the world progresses only by dint of countless attempts to grope its way.[3]

In themselves, these two new dimensions (and others, too, which derive from them) have no direct effect on *the axes* of

1. Offered for professional theological comment. (Note by Père Teilhard.)
2. Not that this means without summit or ending. (Note by Père Teilhard).
3. This is not accidental but of the essence of the process. 'Organicity' and 'atomicity', understood in this sense, are simply the physical attributes necessarily associated with the metaphysical nature of participated being. (Note by Père Teilhard.)

Christian dogma; but if the unity essential to all interior life is to be preserved, it is obviously essential that, both in the system it constructs and the form in which it presents it, theological thought be expressed (qualitatively and quantitatively) in a way that will harmonize with those dimensions. *Homogeneity* (of medium and scale) is (with *coherence*, of which it is simply an aspect) the first condition of all truth.

Nowhere, perhaps, do the necessity, the possibility, and the advantages of such an adjustment stand out more clearly than in the case of the theory of original sin.

II. STATEMENT OF THE PROBLEM

It is no exaggeration to say that, in the form in which it is still commonly presented today, original sin is at the moment one of the chief obstacles that stand in the way of the intensive and extensive progress of Christian thought. An embarrassment or a stumbling-block to the well-meaning but undecided, and at the same time a refuge for the narrow-minded, the *story* of the Fall, as we can see for ourselves, is nullifying the attempt to introduce, as is so essential, a fully human and humanizing Christian *Weltanschauung*. Almost every time I have had occasion publicly to defend the rightful claims and the superiority of a Christian optimism, I have been asked the same innocent or anxious question by the most well-disposed of my audience: 'And original sin – what about that?'

This is obviously an unhealthy situation, and it is all the more annoying in that all that is needed to reverse it completely is the correction in our usual representations of the Fall of a simple error in perspective. What it amounts to is this: In its allegedly traditional form, original sin is generally presented as a 'serial' event, linking up (with an earlier and a later) *inside* history. Yet, for conclusive physical and theological reasons, surely we should treat it, on the contrary, as a reality which belongs to the trans-historic order, affecting (like a colour or a dimension) the whole of our experiential vision of the world.

In this essay I hope to show that this is indeed so; and that once that correction has been made, the conflict between original sin and modern thought disappears so completely that a dogma, at present such an intellectual brake, is suddenly seen to allow us an inner freedom of flight.

III. ORIGINAL SIN, A GENERAL CONDITION OF HISTORY

It is the unanimous opinion of theologians (I believe) that the necessary and sufficient reagent for the existence of original sin in the world is death.[4] That is why, quite logically, the unhappy originators of *retrogressive evolution* try to date the Fall before any known fossil, that is to say in the Pre-Cambrian. Yet, if we are to get to the bottom, not, perhaps, of death itself, in the strict sense of the word, but of its roots, should we not look much further back – infinitely further back, as far as the first origin of things? Consider a moment: Why do living beings die, if not in virtue of the tendency to disintegration essential to every corpuscular structure? Taken in the widest and most fundamental sense of the word, death (that is, disintegration) begins in truth to become apparent as early as the atom. Being built into the very physico-chemical nature of matter, all it does is to express in its own way the structural atomicity of the universe. It is impossible, therefore, to escape from the 'mortal' (and in consequence from the influence or domain of original sin) without escaping from the world itself. Located and tracked down in nature by its specific effect, death,

4. Man's death, pre-eminently, of course; but in consequence *all* death – since, by the inexorable demands of physical homogeneity, man could not have been *alone* in a system of essentially mortal animals in escaping organic decomposition. (Note by Père Teilhard.)

original sin cannot therefore be assigned to any particular place or time. What it does do (as I said earlier) is to affect and infect the whole of time and space. If there is an original sin in the world, it can only be and have been everywhere in it and always, from the earliest of the nebulae to be formed as far as the most distant. This is what science tells us; and, by a most reassuring coincidence, this is what is even now being confirmed (if we carry them to their logical conclusion) by the most orthodox requirements of Christology.

We are not going too far if we say that the most essential aim and criterion of Christian orthodoxy can be reduced to this one point: to maintain Christ *to the measure of and at the head of creation*. However vast the world is found to be, the figure of the risen Christ must *embrace the world*. That, since the time of St John and St Paul, has been the fundamental rule of theology.[5] I wonder, has the direct corollary of this first principle been sufficiently noted, as it affects the nature of the 'first Adam'? The radius of Christ's dominant power is, by 'definition', the radius of the Redemption. Nobody contests this major premise. What would happen then (from the Christological point of view) if original sin were confined to its former scale in our modern view of historical cosmogenesis? If, that is, it were still regarded as an accident that occurred towards the end of the Tertiary period in one corner of the planet earth? It would mean, obviously, that, *directly*, *organically* and *formally*, Christ's power could not extend beyond, could not fill more than, one short slender fibre in the universe which envelops us. In legal title – juridically – Christ could still, it is true, be declared (in virtue of his divine dignity) master of the other cosmic sectors; but he would no longer be, in the full physical sense intended by St Paul, he '*in*

5. St Paul himself in the Epistle to the Romans (9:5) speaks of Adam as essentially related to Christ. This point of view must dominate all theological treatment of the nature of original sin.

quo omnia constant'.[6] From which it follows, on this further ground, that we are once more obliged (not on this occasion as a consequence of the revealed universality of Christ's influence) to consider the phenomenon of the Fall: what we now have to investigate is how it might be conceived or imagined, not as an isolated fact, but as a general condition affecting the whole of history.

Our attempt to do so is all the more warranted, we should note, in that the same obligation to rethink the dogma of original sin is imposed on us from a third quarter of human thought: it comes not from science, nor from theology, but from Scripture. The most recent advances in exegesis insist that what we should look for in the first chapters of Genesis is not 'visual' information about man's *history* but teaching about his *nature*.

So we have a clear road ahead.

IV. A FIRST WAY OF CONCEIVING A TRANS-HISTORIC ORIGINAL SIN: THE SINFUL ORIGIN OF THE MULTIPLE (FIGURE 1)

A first line of thought, if we are trying to picture to ourselves an original sin pan-cosmic in nature, is that explored many years ago by the Alexandrian School.[7] This leads to conceiving the process involving the Fall and its developments as follows:

a. Creation (instantaneous) of a perfect human creature (mankind), the first Adam, whom it would be quite useless, more-

---

6. 'In whom all things hold together' (Col. 1:17).

7. Had it not already been done, it would be interesting to follow up similar indications in the Greek Fathers – as, for example, in that homily in which St Gregory of Nazianzus (or is it of Nyssa?) explains the expulsion from Eden as the fall in a 'denser' form of life. I have an idea that the same views were re-adopted and taught at Louvain some few years ago. (Note by Père Teilhard.)

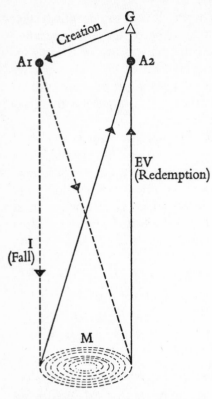

Figure 1. 'Alexandrian' Type of Cosmogenesis. G, God. A1, The first Adam, pre-cosmic, created by an instantaneous act, and complete. M, Multiple (produced by the Fall, i.e. secondary and sinful). A2, The second Adam (Christ). I, Cone of involution in the multiple. EV, Cone of evolution and redemption, forming the cosmos of our experience.

over (we shall be seeing why), to attempt to describe or count. *The Eden phase.*

b. Disobedience, in some form.

c. Fall into the multiple (i.e. producing the multiple). *Precosmic phase of involution.*

d. Redemptive reascent, through progressive reorganization and reunification, towards and in the second Adam. *Cosmic, historical phase of evolution.*

In this scheme, the general conditions required, as we have seen, for the solution of the problem of the Fall both by the nature of the world and by Christology, are abundantly fulfilled: lost in the cone of cosmic 'reascent' (and so incapable of seeing our road down) we see the universe only in the form of an evolution which starts from the multiple – with no place for Eden or its inhabitants – and with death present everywhere and since all time; and, in this system, Christ's operation is quite truly co-extensive with the entire world.

The solution therefore holds good. There are a number of reasons, however, which make it not completely satisfactory to me.

a. First, the whole of the extra-cosmic part of the story has 'an arbitrary and fanciful' ring. It takes us into the realm of pure imagination.

b. Secondly, and much more seriously, the *instantaneous* creation of the first Adam seems to me an incomprehensible type of operation – unless the word simply covers the absence of any attempt at explanation.

c. Finally, if we accept the hypothesis of a *single*, *perfect* being put to the test *on only one occasion*, the likelihood of the Fall is so slight that one can only regard the Creator as having been extremely unlucky.

That is why I have always been attracted by a second type of solution, which I must now explain. It would seem at first to have less classical backing than the first, but I find it more elegant, more rational, more coherent – and, most of all, more worthy of the world and of God.

V. SECOND LINE OF THOUGHT: EVOLUTIVE CREATION AND STATISTICAL ORIGIN OF EVIL (FIGURE 2)

In the 'Alexandrian' explanation described above, the multiple from which evolution emerges is both *secondary* and *sinful from its origin*: it represents in fact (an idea that smacks of Manicheanism and the Hindu metaphysical systems) broken and pul-

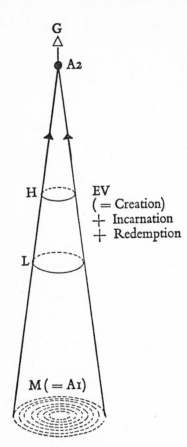

Figure 2. 'Modern' Type of Cosmogenesis.
G, God. A2, Christ (the second Adam). M, Multiple (primordial, non-sinful, 'creatable' form (*'creabilis'*, not *'creanda'*)[1] of non-being, functional equivalent of the 'first Adam', source of statistical evil). H, Level at which human freedom (and sin) appears. L, Level at which life and suffering appear. EV, Evolutive cone (of Creation, Incarnation, and Redemption).

[1] Creatable, not necessarily destined to be created.

Within the figure:
G
A2
H
EV
(= Creation)
+ Incarnation
+ Redemption
L
M (= A1)

verized unity. Starting from a very much more modern and completely different point of view, let us assert, as our original postulate, that, the multiple (that is, *non-being*, if taken in the pure state) being the only rational form of a creatable (*creabile*) nothingness, the creative act is comprehensible only as a gradual process of arrangement and unification.[8] In virtue of

8.Which amounts to accepting that *to create is to unite*. And, indeed, there is nothing to prevent our holding that *union creates*. To the objection that union presupposes already existing elements, I shall answer that physics

this postulate, the history of the world (and even of every possible world) can be represented symbolically as in Figure 2. In that diagram the right-hand half of Figure 1 can immediately be recognized, but with this difference that in Figure 2 the basic multiple represents not the debris of a pulverized being, but the original, essential form of participated being.

But this is still not all. If we examine the structure and properties of the cosmic cone so defined it is not long before we realize that in this case the primordial multiple is in no way directly sinful; on the other hand, since its gradual unification entails a multitude of tentative probings in the immensities of space-time, it cannot escape (from the moment it ceases to be 'nothing') being permeated by suffering and error. *Statistically*, in fact, in the case of a system which is in process of organization, it is absolutely inevitable ('fatalistically determined'): (1) that local disorders appear during the process ('*necessarium est ut adveniant scandala*'),[9] and (2) that, from level to level, collective states of disorder result from these elementary disorders (because of the organically interwoven nature of the cosmic stuff). Above the level of life, this entails suffering, and, starting with man, it becomes sin.[10]

Very well: once this point is understood and accepted, must it not be clear (unless I am very much mistaken) that, from the point of view of the Fall, the less elaborate universe of Figure 2 meets all the most immediately urgent requirements of

---

has just shown us (in the case of mass) that experientially (and for all the protests of 'common sense') the moving object exists only as the product of its motion. (Note by Père Teilhard.)

9. 'It is necessary that temptations come': the exact text (Matt. 18:7) is '*Necesse est enim ut veniant scandala*'.

10. This clear-cut statement avoids the ambiguity of certain expressions which might result in evil appearing to be in man the pure statistical result of a process of evolution.

cosmology and theology just as well as, and even better than, the world of Figure 1?

In such a universe:

1. The evidence of science is necessarily, and always will be, respected, since the experiential background of dogma coincides with that of evolution.

2. The problem (the intellectual problem) of evil disappears. In this picture, physical suffering and moral transgressions are inevitably introduced into the world not because of some deficiency in the creative act but by the very structure of participated being: in other words they are introduced as the *statistically inevitable by-product* of the unification of the multiple. In consequence they contradict neither the power of God nor his goodness. Is the game worth the candle? Everything depends on the *final* value and beatitude of the universe – a point on which we may well trust ourselves to God's wisdom.[11]

3. Finally, and most important of all, the theology of salvation would appear to be perfectly respected and justified. It is true that in this explanation original sin ceases to be an isolated *act* and becomes a *state* (affecting the human mass as a whole, as a result of an endless stream of transgressions punctuating mankind in the course of time). Yet even this, far from weakening the dogmatic characteristics of the Fall, intensifies them. In the first place, redemption is indeed universal, since it corrects a state of affairs (the universal presence of disorder) which is tied up with the most basic structure of the universe in process of creation. Secondly, individual baptism retains, and in an even more emphatic form, its full justification. Looked at in this way, each new soul waken-

11. In a general way, this amounts to saying that the problem of evil, insoluble in the case of a static universe (i.e. a 'cosmos'), no longer arises in the case of a (multiple) evolutive universe (i.e. a cosmogenesis). It is strange that so simple a truth should still be so little perceived and stated. (Note by Père Teilhard.)

ing into life is integrally contaminated by the totalized influence of all transgressions, past, present, and still to come,
which by statistical necessity are inevitably spread throughout
the human whole as it proceeds towards sanctification.[12] In
each soul there is something which needs to be purified.

On first consideration, as I was saying, one might fear that
the representation of the original Fall offered in preference
here was only a device for respecting an irksome dogma
verbally, while emptying it of its traditional content. The
truth, however, is that the more one thinks about it, the more
one sees that while the transposition brings the notion of
original sin completely into line with a modern view of the
universe,[13] it entirely respects Christian thought and the
customary Christian approach – the only corrective it contributes, in short, being to substitute a collective 'matrix' and
a collective heredity for the womb of our mother Eve. And
this, incidentally, has the further result of releasing us from the
necessity (progressively more unacceptable) of having, illogically, to derive the whole human race from one single couple.[14]

N.B. Whereas, in a universe of the 'Alexandrian' type
(Figure 1), creation and redemption correspond to two independent and distinct operations, it should be noted that in

12. We may note as particularly harmful among these transgressions: (a)
the *first* transgressions committed on earth (committed with minimum
consciousness, but with maximum effect on a nascent psychism); (b) perhaps
(if, in the area of freedom, the future can cause a reaction in the past) certain
final refusals of obedience on the part of mankind after attaining maturity
(maximum consciousness and responsibility); and finally (c) for each individual the offences committed in his own social group and as the product
of his own particular heredity. (Note by Père Teilhard.)

13. Since original sin then becomes a combined effect of atomicity
(statistical disorder) and organicity (general contamination of the human
mass). (Note by Père Teilhard.)

14. The theological side of the explanation offered here has been upheld
in Lyons by Père Rondet. (Note by Père Teilhard.)

the second sort of world (Figure 2) Creation, Incarnation and Redemption are seen to be no more than the three complementary aspects of one and the same process: Creation (*because it is unifying*) entailing a certain immersion of the Creator in his work, and at the same time (*because* it is necessarily productive of evil as a secondary statistical effect) entailing a certain redemptive compensation. I have met the objection to this that everything works out too simply and too clearly for the explanation to be sound! To which I answer that in the explanation offered the mystery is most certainly not destroyed but simply restored to its true place (that is, right at the summit and in the whole), so that it is not precisely either Creation, or Incarnation, or Redemption, in their mechanism, but 'pleromization': I mean the mysterious 'repletive' (if not 'completive') relationship which links the first being with participated being.[15]

Unpublished, Paris, 15 November 1947.

15. For the 'completive' relationship between the first being and participated being, see the passage quoted from Pierre de Bérulle, below, p. 225, n. 3.

THE CHRISTIAN
PHENOMENON

IN our first approach to a general view of Christianity (that is, apart from any theological consideration) we see it empirically at this moment as one of the principal, and even in fact (if we except Islam, which is no more than a backward-looking revival of Judaism – and neo-humanist Marxism, which seems destined to become Christianized) as the most recent of the religious currents to appear historically in the thinking layers of the noosphere. No one dreams of refusing to this collective movement of vision and belief, already two thousand years old, the signal honour of having served as the matrix of our western civilization – and that, in all probability, means of the whole human civilization of tomorrow. Could anyone, for example, say to what extent the gospel message, not only in a potential form but as a legacy, permeates the most Stalinist materialism? Everyone is prepared to admit the importance of Christianity *in the past*; but what about the present? and still more the future? Surely, after two thousand years of existence the Christian movement (like so many others before it) must be showing some signs of growing old and wearing out? Is the Christian God still climbing to the meridian – or is he not rather about to set on our horizon?

This is a poignantly tragic question – *and for everybody*: for nobody can say to what degree the sun of Christ is still continuing, here and now in the twentieth century, to guide us and warm us – without our realizing it. What deep repercussions would there be in us – among us, too – should the disappearance of that sun plunge us into night?[1]

1. The great fear (so threatening to our nervous equilibrium) overhanging the world at this moment is undoubtedly cosmic rather than political; by

In what follows I hope to be able to show how, by two sights taken at a sufficient distance to eliminate every proximate cause of error, we may find it possible to determine the orbit in question: how, on sound objective evidence, we may recognize that the heavenly star above us is not sinking but is continuing its ascending course, and seems destined to do so up to a zenith that coincides with that of terrestrial thought itself – through a perpetual renewal of its sharpness and brilliance.

This is our first sight, or consideration: in Christianity, in the form of an ever more explicitly defined faith in the existence of a divine centre of universal convergence, it is the whole monotheist current which is now arriving at mystical maturity.

And the second consideration: in the process of general noogenesis (and more precisely still in that of planetary anthropogenesis), in which we are daily finding ourselves to be more deeply involved, it is monotheism (in its most advanced form) which alone seems to be psychologically capable, when it really comes to the point, of maintaining the progress of evolution.

These two facts, it is clear, combine together and confirm one another, to guarantee to the Christian phenomenon an importance and a value that are exactly co-extensive, both in intensity and in duration, with the predictable developments of mankind.

I. CHRISTIANITY AND MONOTHEISM

Both *a priori* and *a posteriori*, monotheism has every sort of right to be regarded as one of the principal elementary forms (if not the sole primitive form) of religious feeling. The fact

---

that I mean that it is caused by the darkening of a de-divinized heaven, much more than by the rise of any atomic wave. (Note by Père Teilhard.)

is (as we can tell from ourselves) that when man has newly arrived at reflection, no movement is more instinctive to him than to breathe life into and to anthropomorphize in the form of a great someone *all the Other* whose existence, influence and menace he finds all around him.[2] It is, indeed, at this particular stage of worship, according to some observers, that the least socially evolved peoples of the earth are still arrested.

All this is most probably true; but it does not alter the fact – not by any means – that the notion of a single great and supreme master of the world is, in this respect, like every other profound psychic intuition or aspiration: in the course of a long advance towards maturity, it could have (or even must have) passed from an initial simplicity marked by vagueness and indetermination ('pre-monotheism') to an ever-higher simplicity marked by elaboration and clarity ('eu-monotheism', or evolved monotheism), whose highest terms still lie far ahead of us.

As normally happens with 'speciation' or phylogenesis, the first stages of this religious development cannot be distinctly observed, either in their mystical modalities or in their ethnical and geographical distribution. On the other hand, one point is well established, that (three or four thousand years ago) what was to become the powerful main stem of modern monotheism emerged unmistakably in those amazingly progressive regions which extend from the Nile to the Euphrates: from the warmth released by Egypt, Iran and Greece sprang *the Judaeo-Christian branch*.

Once this specially favoured axis is completely individualized, two major, and more or less simultaneous, transformations of it can readily be detected in the biblical narratives: one producing universalization, and the other 'amorization'. In his

2. And (in spite of anything urged by Father W. Schmidt and his followers) without having to introduce any divine 'revelation'. (Note by Père Teilhard.)

first recorded origins, the Hebrew Yahweh is still only the chief and the most powerful of the 'gods'; and his power is concentrated upon a single chosen people, with a preference that still has disturbing aspects. In fact, it called for an effort that was to last for several centuries (until the Christian revolution, that is) for the cosmic potentialities of the Demiurge of Genesis finally to be defined and humanized in the worship of a God who was not only the awful master but the loving and lovable Father of all men without exception.

And even then, contrary to a too prevalent opinion, the process was far from being complete.

For, speaking with complete and profound respect for Christ's human words, one cannot fail to see that the Judaeo-Christian faith is still expressed (and necessarily) in the gospel texts in terms of a typically Neolithic symbolism: of the age when a mankind (and, more widely, a world) was built, from heaven above to the village below, on the model (and almost on the scale) of the family and the ploughed field. In such a universe, how can one conceive, without psychological contradiction, that monotheism could have been expressed other than in terms of God as the great head of the family and supreme owner of the inhabited world?

It is just this mental framework or background from which our modern consciousness is now emerging more and more completely. All around us, through all the avenues of experience and thought, the universe is irresistibly knitting itself together organically and genetically. In such conditions, how could the Father-God of two thousand years ago (still a cosmos-God) fail to be transformed imperceptibly (the very fact of our worship hastening the process) into a cosmogenesis-God – in other words into some focus or animating principle of an *evolutive* creation in which our own individual condition is much less that of a servant who works than that of an element that is united?

This, if I am right, indeed represents here and now one of the principal characteristics of the phenomenon of man. We might have had the impression that the stream of religious invention which flows around us and in our own selves had for a long time been halted and stabilized in its highest possible expression. Now we see that this is not true. On one side we have mystical currents of the Eastern type which still persist in seeking unity in an act of identification, by diffusion, with the distended totality of the cosmic sphere; and confronting it, we are witnessing, in the form of a Christology extended to the new dimensions of time and space, the rise of an extreme expression of monotheism from the phyletic depths of Christianity – along, that is, the Roman Catholic axis: Monotheism, no longer based simply on rulership but on convergence, at the summit of which (through love's victory over the cosmic forces of multiplicity and dispersion) a universal centre of things radiates and (in the scriptural expression) is 'pleromized'.

And now we may shift our attention for a moment from the subtle but profound change which reaches to the heart of modern mystical feeling and affects the very complexion of God, and give some thought to what is meanwhile happening in the general current of human consciousness.

II. MONOTHEISM AND NEO-HUMANISM

In the constructive and fruitful debate which still divides neo-Darwinists and neo-Lamarckians in the biological field, it is curious to note how unconcernedly both the opposing schools equally take for granted without discussion a certain mainspring or dynamism without which the evolutive mechanisms they imagine would inevitably be as inert as an engine with an empty petrol tank. It is, in fact, clear that in both cases – whether the transformation of species is effected from outside (by natural selection) or from inside (as a result of invention) –

we must imagine, at the heart of the animate being, a certain polarization or preference in favour of 'survival', if not even of 'super-living'. If a living substance is completely neutral and without tension, then no stimulation of its environment, no statistical influence of large numbers, can get to work on it at all. Just as the expansion of the universe (if we accept it?) presupposes a certain repellent action between material particles, which originated in the explosion of the 'primitive atom' – so, if we are to maintain the efflorescence of the biosphere (and here there is no need for a question-mark), we are inevitably obliged to rely on the primordial existence, and the progressively more marked emergence throughout the ages, of a certain *evolutionary pressure*.

It would be over-ingenuous to seek for a well-defined expression, valid at all levels of biogenesis, for this 'evolutionary pressure' which is the ultimate mainspring of all vital movement. On the other hand, starting from the critical point of reflection, that is to say once we enter the domain of man, its inner nature is decisively 'psychized' in a perfectly clear and familiar form – it is what we may simply call the *zest for living*.

The zest for living . . .

For the last twelve years, there has hardly been a single lecture or a single article dealing with man in which I have not felt more and more imperatively obliged to emphasize the vital (though nearly always overlooked) function of this fundamental energy: without it, under the most violent pressures of the planetary milieu, and in spite of the lavish assistance of all the requisite material resources, the magnificent human drive would grind to a miserable halt – if it should be so unfortunate as *no longer to have any desire* to carry on. Dreaded though it is, the intervention of ill-will and ill-luck (statistically determined by the alternate or combined operation of selection or invention) does not seem to me (to judge from the past) to be a serious threat to the future of the thinking world. Once the evolutive movement has been launched and is under way nothing, it would appear, can then prevent life on our earth from attaining the maximum possible degree of its development: nothing – except, indeed, the general instantaneous slackening-off that could be brought about by the fatal shock of a great disillusionment.

This is something we must constantly bear in mind ever more clearly. If man, still embryonic, is to reach the adult stage, he must, absolutely and as a first priority, retain until the very end his desire to arrive at his own ultimate term – and this in spite of the emergence in him of ever more acute critical faculties. In other words, if the universe is not to disappoint (and thereby *stifle*) the thought to which it has given birth, it must satisfy certain basic structural conditions.

And if you ask what these conditions are, I can distinguish two of them – these not so much corresponding, as one might imagine, to the attractions, greater or not so great, of the present moment, as both linked together to the dimensions and colouring of the most distant future. Imagine (if you will pardon my using the comparison once again) a group of miners trapped by accident deep underground. The survivors will obviously make up their minds to climb back along the gallery in which they are collected only if they can assume the existence above them of (1) a way out, and (2) a way out that leads to air and light. It is just the same with a generation (our own) wihch is suddenly confronted with the reality of having to make a long and arduous effort in order to reach the higher, and ever receding, limit of the human. It would be useless, I maintain, to tell such a generation to press on, if we had grounds to suspect that the world is hermetically closed ahead of us, or that it opens out only into something that is 'inhuman' (or sub-human). A *total* death in which the evolutive fruit of our planetary effort would be lost for all time and for all of us; or again, which could come to the same thing, a weakened or distorted form of survival which would not contain what is most valuable in the spiritually unifying vision with which life urges us to co-operate: it seems to me psychologically *certain* that either of these two gloomy prospects would be sufficient in itself for the lightning poison of boredom, fear and heart-sickness to strike, without hope of cure, at the marrow of our active energy.

The more life is individualized, the more it finds an absolute *irreversible* need in itself.

Expressed in positive terms, this means simply that the only form of universe compatible with the presence and persistence on earth of a thought, is a system psychically convergent on some cosmic focus of conservation and ultra-personalization.

It is a categorical biological demand in which unexpectedly we meet again, in its most evolved and also most modern form, the great monotheistic aspiration of all times.

III. CHRISTIANITY AND THE FUTURE

Thus, without our really appreciating it, a vast psychological event is taking place, at this very moment, in the noosphere: what it amounts to is the meeting of the Above with the Ahead; in other words, the confluence, along the Christian axis, of the canalized stream of the ancient mysticisms and the newer but rapidly swelling torrent of the sense of evolution. The anticipation of a transcendent superhuman and the anticipation of an immanent ultrahuman have run together, and these two forms of faith are providing one another with a boundless illumination and reinforcement. In very truth, I am convinced that it is not premature to see in so marvellously balanced an interplay the order in which the mysterious planetary process of hominization is destined henceforth to be effected until its consummation.[3]

3. This does not, of course, exclude the possible appearance in human

The more one studies this situation, the more, and the more forcefully, there comes to mind a curiously interesting analogy between what one might call *the religious state* of the world today and *the zoological state* of the earth at the end of the Tertiary. At that time (that is, about a million years ago) an informed observer examining the multitude of large African Primates might have been able to recognize, from countless anatomical and psychical indications, that a particular hominoid line or fascicle contained in itself the promises of the future. Similarly, I would say, it is indisputable (if we know how to look) that a difference and a radical advance can easily be distinguished, which permanently set the 'Christian phenomenon' apart from every single one of the other 'religious phenomena' among which it appeared but which it has continually, ever since its origins, been striving to shake off.

Today every other religion is mercilessly halted in its stride by the obstacle of a universe that has become so organic and so demanding that it outruns or disheartens most of the great mystical intuitions of the past; Christianity, however, rises effortlessly above this situation, carried along by the very conditions, so profoundly changed, of thought and action to which the most eminent of its rivals cannot succeed in accommodating themselves.

It is no exaggeration to say that, because of its quite special ultra-monotheism, the religion of Christ is not only proving in experience that it can stand up to the new temperatures and new tensions produced in the human mind by the appearance of the idea of evolution – it is also finding in this transformed domain an optimum environment for development and communication. And for this reason it is establishing itself as hence-

---

consciousness of some *third* axis, as yet unsuspected, besides the Above and the Ahead – were it only as the result of some form of contact being made with other thinking planets. (Note by Père Teilhard.)

forth the *definitive religion* of a world which has suddenly become conscious of its dimensions and its course, both in space and in time.

From this it follows that if we carry ourselves in imagination not a million years backward but a million years ahead, through the opening folds of the cosmos, and ask ourselves in conclusion (with maybe a touch of anxiety) what we can expect will remain of Christianity at that distant period, we can quite safely say at least this:

'At such a depth of the future, and considering the present rate of anthropogenesis, it would be idle to try to decide what forms will have been assumed, either by the liturgy and canon law, or by theological conceptions of the supernatural and of revelation, or by the attitude of moralists to the great problems of eugenics and scientific research – quite apart from the fact that in a million years' time many of the historical problems which are still so important to us will long have been solved or have disappeared. There is nothing we can say about those matters. On the other hand, one thing is certain. If, when that time comes, mankind (as we are assuming) is still growing in stature (which means reflecting upon itself) it will be a proof that the zest for life has not ceased to flourish in it. And that presupposes that, with its disclosing of a pole ever more attractive to the convergent efforts of noogenesis, a more and more fully "Christified" monotheism will *always be at hand* (even if everything else has to change) to renew the atmosphere of the universe and to "amorize" evolution.'

Unpublished, Paris, 10 May 1950.

MONOGENISM
AND MONOPHYLETISM:
AN ESSENTIAL DISTINCTION

THE encyclical *Humani Generis* has introduced a new discussion with a great deal of high feeling and confusion, of the problem of the historical representation of the origins of man. It is an appropriate occasion to emphasize once more the essential difference between the two notions (still too often regarded as synonymous) of:

Mono- and poly-*genism*: one or a number of original human *couples*.

Mono- and poly-*phyletism*: one or a number of *branches* (or phyla) at the foundation of mankind.

First Principle

Since it is impossible (and will always, no doubt, remain impossible) for science to magnify the palaeontological past sufficiently for *individuals* to be distinguished – that is, for us to recognize very far back in the past anything but *populations* – it follows that monogenism and polygenism are in reality *purely theological notions*, introduced for dogmatic reasons, but (being experimentally unverifiable) extra-scientific by nature.

Second Principle

This amounts to saying that when a scientist, as a scientist, recognizes the unity of the human species, he has no intention at all of affirming the existence of a single original couple: all he is saying is that man represents zoologically a single *stem* –

whatever, apart from that, may be the numerical density and the morphological complexity of that stem at its beginning.

In science one cannot speak of monogenism or polygenism, but *only* of monophyletism and polyphyletism.

The theologian, in consequence, is to some degree free to assume what seems to him to be dogmatically necessary inside the area of indetermination created by the imperfect nature of our scientific vision of the past. *Directly*, the scientist *cannot* prove that the hypothesis of an individual Adam must be rejected. *Indirectly*, however, he may judge that this hypothesis is rendered scientifically untenable by all we believe we know so far of the biological laws of 'speciation' (or 'genesis of species').

a. In the first place, I mean, the simultaneous appearance of a mutation in one single couple seems infinitely improbable to a geneticist; but what is more, it raises the question for him of whether, even if it were effected in the case of man, so limited a mutation would have any chance at all of propagating itself.

b. Secondly (and this is much more serious) what the monogenism of the theologians demands is not only the uniqueness of an original couple – but the sudden appearance of two individuals *fully complete in their specific development* from the first moment. At the very least, the Adam of the theologians must have been from the outset a *Homo sapiens*. Properly speaking, he must have been *born adult*.[1] And used in conjunction, those two words are meaningless for modern science. *Contra leges naturae*.[2]

This leaves us with two alternatives:

Either there will be an essential change tomorrow in the scientific laws of speciation (which is highly improbable).

Or (which seems fully in conformity with recent advances

---

1. If he was to be capable of bearing the responsibility for original sin. (Note by Père Teilhard.)

2. 'Against the laws of nature.'

in exegesis) theologians will somehow come to realize that, in a universe as organically structured as that of which we are now becoming conscious, a solidarity of man, much closer even than that which they seek in 'the bosom of Mother Eve', is readily provided for them by the extraordinary internal cohesion of a world which, all around us, is in a state of cosmo- and anthropo-genesis.

Unpublished, Paris, 1950.

WHAT THE WORLD
IS LOOKING FOR FROM THE
CHURCH OF GOD AT
THIS MOMENT:
A GENERALIZING AND A
DEEPENING OF THE MEANING
OF THE CROSS

I. INTRODUCTION: WHY THIS IS WRITTEN

FOUR years ago I sent to Rome, under the title *The Heart of the Problem (Le Cœur du Problème)*, a short report in which I tried to make my superiors understand what seemed to me to be the real source of modern religious restlessness. What I said was the fruit of many long years spent, as a result of exceptional circumstances, in the most intimate contact, *simultaneously*, with the world of science and the world of faith; and the source I refer to is the irresistible rise in the human sky, through all the avenues of thought and action, of an evolutive God of the Ahead – hostile, at first glance, to the transcendent God of the Above whom Christianity offers for our worship.

'So long as the Church neglects, by means of a refashioned Christology (all the elements of which are available to us), to solve the apparent conflict that henceforth exists between the traditional God of revelation and the "new" God of evolution, so long, too,' I wrote in that report, 'will there be increasing distress not only on the fringe of the believing world but at its very core; and, *pari passu*, Christianity's power to attract and convert will grow less.'

In what I then wrote I made no claim to encroach on established authority. Nevertheless, it was the evidence of an observer who had by accident made his way into those deep-lying human zones into which officialdom normally has no opportunity of penetrating, let alone of being able to understand what goes on in them.

This in itself might have given my words a claim to attention.

The answer that I received from Rome was that my diagnosis did not coincide with the ideas currently accepted in the Eternal City.

And since then, as we all know, the religious 'schizophrenia' from which we suffer has constantly grown more marked.

Once again, then, for time is short, I am going to try to make myself understood. But this time, for the sake of greater clarity, I shall avoid any symbolic or abstract expression, and restate the problems (and perhaps the solution) in the unmistakably palpable and concrete form *they assume for me* when I look at them in the context of, and from a starting-point in, *the meaning of the Cross*.

This means, moreover, that I must first draw attention again to an event to whose obviousness some minds are still oddly closed: I mean the gradual and irresistible introduction, as part and parcel of our modern civilization, of a radically refashioned conception of man and mankind.

II. PRELIMINARY OBSERVATION: THE APPEARANCE AND NATURE OF A CONTEMPORARY NEO-HUMANISM

There was a time (the heyday of Scholasticism) when the greatest minds debated, without reaching any conclusion, the problem of whether one should be 'realist' or 'nominalist'.

An infallible sign of a question that is wrongly phrased . . .

Today (at least so far as living beings are concerned) scientific evolutionism has, without any difficulty, given new and clearer expression to the problem of universals, simply by introducing the notion of 'phyletic species'. 'Philosophers' are welcome to carry on their futile arguments about the general idea of Cat or Dog. In fact, the only general 'feline' or 'canine' entity which exists and matters *in natura rerum,*[1] we now know, is a certain population, derived from one and the same stem, and expressible in a certain statistical curve of variability.

Besides (or rather *instead of*) the abstract universal and the concrete universal, there is the *genetic universal.*

From this new point of view, we are obliged to recognize that 'the idea of man' (and this is true of all the other animal categories) has lost for us, in a first phase, all its mystery – and much of its aura of Platonism.

On the other hand, and balancing this, we have immediately to add that, in a second phase, this same concept of man has been (or is being, at least) restored, on experiential grounds, to its former dignity; and this in two ways.

In the first place, it is becoming more and more imperative to recognize, on sound scientific grounds, that the appearance on earth, with the Quaternary, of reflected consciousness (thought) introduced a new phase in the history of the biosphere. Man, zoologically classifiable as a mammal of the order of Primates, represents primarily, in fact, the appearance on the planet of *a second species of life* (or, to put it in another way, of 'a second-degree life').

Secondly (a situation which is less generally recognized as yet, but which science will before long be obliged to accept *also*) this second-species (or reflected) life is by nature of a *convergent habit.* For fundamental biological reasons, man cannot exist without covering the earth; and he cannot cover the earth without totalizing and centring on himself ever more fully. So strong is this compulsion that in man (unique in nature in this respect) the species does not diverge and dissipate,

1. 'In nature.'

but converges progressively more closely upon itself with the passage of time.

In the case of man, and man *alone* (because he is *reflective*), the genetic universal tends to consolidate, as far as it can carry the process, in super-personal unity.

These new views on man's unique nature, I repeat, are not yet generally expressed in science, nor with equal force; but they derive so directly and so closely from the whole modern scientific *Weltanschauung* that they are beginning, in fact, to colour and permeate all that is conscious (or subconscious, at least) in our own time.

We must make no mistake about this: in spite of the froth of existentialism and Barthianism which has been smothering us during recent years, the basic current in the world at this moment is not heartsick pessimism (whether atheist or religious) but a conquering optimism (as evidenced by the rapid rise of Marxism). It is not only self-centred, grasping ambition directed towards 'well-being'; it is also a collective drive towards 'fuller-being', expected and sought for in the direction of the fulfilment of the zoological group to which we belong.

There was a period of vacillation (the sixteenth to the nineteenth centuries) when it might have seemed that the human was going to disintegrate more and more into autonomous individuals; but today, under the pressure of formidable external and internal determinisms, we are unquestionably finding the sense of the species once again, on a higher plane. This time, it is not slavish adherence to the line of heredity, but the unanimous and concerted drive to reach, all together, some higher stage of life.

The old spirit of the Renaissance and the eighteenth century is dead or obsolete, we must realize: the notion of well-ordered cosmos and of man neatly fitting into the pattern. In its place a new humanism is blossoming in almost every quarter – as an irresistible effect of co-reflection. It is a humanism not of balance, but of movement, in which no value can still hold good – *even, and particularly, in the area of religion* – unless it allows room for the existence of some ultra-human cosmic future and conforms to its demands.

And this brings me to the heart of my subject: the urgent necessity for the Church to lose no time in offering the world a 'new' meaning (an ultra-humanized meaning) of the Cross.

III. CROSS OF EXPIATION, AND CROSS OF EVOLUTION

By its birth, and for all time, Christianity is pledged to the Cross, and dominated by the sign of the Cross. It cannot remain its own self except by identifying itself ever more intensely with the essence of the Cross.

But what exactly is the essence – what is *the true* meaning of the Cross?

In its *elementary* traditional form (as still commonly presented in pious literature, sermons, and even in seminary teaching) the Cross is *primarily* a symbol of atonement and expiation. As such, it expresses and is the medium for a whole psychological complex in which the following elements can be distinctly recognized, at least as tendencies:

a. A catastrophic conception of evil and death, and their dominance in the world, regarded as the natural and chronological consequence of an original transgression.

b. An attitude of mistrust towards man, who, without being exactly mutilated or perverted (theologians get out of this by the device of 'supernatural' gifts), has neither the soundness nor the vigour required for success in his earthly enterprises.

c. And, what is even more symptomatic, a general, and almost Manichean, mistrust of anything which is matter; matter being regarded almost universally much less as a reservoir of spirit than as a principle of fall and corruption.

All this, fortunately and without any doubt, is shot through with the fire of potent love for the crucified God; but it is the fire of a love which is almost exclusively 'ascensional' in type, its most operative and most significant act being always presented in the form of a painful purification and a joyless detachment.

For the neo-humanists we all are now, this soon produces an atmosphere which we find unbreathable, and *it must be changed*.

If the Cross is to reign over an earth that has suddenly awoken to consciousness of a biological movement drawing it ahead, then at all costs and as soon as possible it must (if it is to be able to co-exist with human nature which it claims to save) present itself to us as a sign, not merely of 'escape',[2] but of progress.

It must have for us not merely a purifying but a *driving* brilliance.

Can the Cross be so transformed, *without distortion*? My answer is an emphatic 'Yes'; it can, and it must, if we get right down to the root of the problem, be transformed by what is most traditional in the Christian spirit.

And it can be done in this way: forget for a moment all that I have just said about the classical and 'sub-pessimist' meaning of the Cross. Leaving aside the Cross itself for the

2. The escape (Père Teilhard uses the English word) which is rejected here is that which, on the ground of the 'redemptive' value of suffering, would dispense us from fighting with all our strength against evil. Meeting with God, on the other hand, presupposes constant co-operation with his creative will. 'The optimum of my "communion in resignation" necessarily coincides with the maximum of fidelity to the human task', Père Teilhard writes in *Le Milieu Divin* (Collins, London, 1960, p. 73; *The Divine Milieu*, Harper, New York, 1960, pp. 65-6).

time being, let us consider the second factor in the modern religious conflict – evolution, now so familiar to us.

Reduced to its most essential features, this forceful reality presents itself to our experience as possessing the following characteristics:

a. In virtue of its 'arranging' nature, it calls for hard work: it is 'effort'.

b. As a statistical effect of chances, it can advance in its tentative constructions only by leaving behind it at all levels (inorganic, organic, and psychic) a long trail of disorder, suffering and error ('evolutive' evil).

c. By the very structure of the process of biological evolution (organic senescence, genetic substitution, metamorphosis) it entails death.

d. Finally, by a necessity that is at once psychological and dynamic, it requires at its peak (when once it has reached the 'reflective' level) a magnetic principle, 'amorizing' the entire functioning of the universe.

We must soak ourselves in the feeling for these four fundamental conditions which determine the very atmosphere of the new world to which we awaken as we become conscious of the moving organicity of the things which make up our world.

And then, when we have really grasped this new evidence, let us turn back to the Cross – and look at a crucifix.

What we see nailed to the wood – suffering, dying, freeing – is that really still the God of original sin? Is it? or is it not the God of evolution?

Or rather, is not the God of evolution – the God for whom our neo-humanism is looking – precisely and simply, taken in the fullest sense of the words and in a generalized form, the very God of expiation?

And this because, if we consider the matter carefully, 'to bear the sins of the guilty world' means precisely, *translated and transposed into terms of cosmogenesis*, 'to bear the weight of a world in a state of evolution'.[3]

In truth (and this is the appeal or evidence I now hope to win attention for in the right quarter) – in truth, the more it has become physically impossible for me to kneel in spirit before a *purely* redemptive Cross, the more passionately I feel drawn to and satisfied by a Cross in which the two components of the future are synthesized: the transcendent and the ultra-human; or, as I said at the beginning, the Above and the Ahead.

Personally, I cannot be blind to the evidence that in the second case (except for one dimension) it is exactly the same Cross which I worship: the same Cross, *but much more true.*

And I feel, and know, that I am not alone in this interior – categorical and final – attitude: there are countless others following the same stream and joining up with me.

CONCLUSION

To sum up in conclusion: in spite of the profound readjustments that are being made in our phenomenal vision of the world, the Cross still stands; it rears itself up ever more erect at the common meeting place of all values and all problems, deep in the heart of mankind. It marks and must continue more than ever to mark the division between what rises and what falls back.

---

3. In view of the present confusion, it should be made plain that 'to bear the weight of a world in evolution' does not minimize the role of sacrifice, but adds to the pain of expiation the more constant and demanding pain of sharing, with full consciousness of man's destiny, in the universal labour which is indispensable to its accomplishment.

Seen in this light, there is even greater force in Christ's summons: 'If any man would come after me, let him deny himself and take up his cross daily and follow me' (Luke 9: 23).

But this is on one condition, and one only: that it expand itself to the dimensions of a new age, and cease to present itself to us as primarily (or even exclusively) the sign of a victory over sin – and so finally attain its fullness, which is to become the dynamic and complete symbol of a universe in a state of personalizing evolution.

Unpublished, New York (Purchase), 14 September 1952.

THE CONTINGENCE OF
THE UNIVERSE AND MAN'S ZEST
FOR SURVIVAL,
OR
HOW CAN ONE RETHINK THE
CHRISTIAN NOTION OF CREATION
TO CONFORM WITH THE LAWS
OF ENERGETICS?

I. PRELIMINARY OBSERVATION:
RELIGIOUS FAITH AND EVOLUTIONARY ENERGY

PROFESSIONAL scientists are now undoubtedly reaching agreement about the true nature of the phenomenon of man. Man used to be regarded as an anomaly in the universe; from now on he is tending to be seen as the extreme point attained at this moment, in the field of our experience, by the combined process of corpuscular arrangement and psychical interiorization sometimes known as 'negative entropy' or 'anti-entropy' – or, more simply, evolution.

'Evolution has not come to a halt, as one might first have thought, in reflective man (in so far as he is reflective): on the contrary (as a result of convergence), it is making a fresh, and more vigorous, start, in the direction of ever higher degrees of co-reflection, in the form of *self-evolution*.'

Such an assertion, there can be no doubt, is now definitively accepted, more or less explicitly, by the majority of scientists; but what many of that majority still seem not to appreciate is the profound change, *dynamic* in order, which is entailed by the incorporation of the human, that is, the reflective, in the progress of evolution.

During its pre-human phase, the vitalization of matter could be regarded (at least as a first general picture) as being fed exclusively, under the influence of chance and natural selection, from the thermodynamic reserves stored on the surface of the earth. By contrast, once the operation is hominized its success demands *in addition* (as we can constantly see in ourselves) the imponderable but determining influence of a certain 'field', psychic in nature, which may be defined as a zest or desire. Without Jean Herzog's passion for the great peaks, there would have been no ascent of Annapurna.

In a system of self-evolution, the energy brought into play is not *only* physical: it appears as a complex magnitude in which two heterogeneous terms are inseparably combined:

a. The first (which can be reckoned in thermodynamic units) can ultimately be reduced to molecular and atomic *attractions*.

b. The second ('measurable' in degrees of arrangement) is experienced by our consciousness in the form of *attractions*.

In other words, if evolution is to continue in a hominized medium, it is physically necessary that man *believe*, as vigorously as possible, in some absolute value possessed by the movement which it is his duty to forward.

In consequence, we now find an unexpected bridge linking experientially two domains apparently so foreign to one another as physical chemistry and religion. Faith is no longer merely an escape route from the world – but the ferment and co-principle of the actual fulfilment of the world. This is an astonishing intellectual eye-opener, no doubt; but, what is even more, it offers an unexpected possibility of satisfying our need to predict and determine, *in the name of energetics*, two general conditions for the future evolution of 'the religious', all during the tens of thousands, or even millions, of years for which the process of hominization has still to last on earth.[1]

1. Père Teilhard is writing as a palaeontologist. He would accept that,

First condition. If man is to reach the natural term of his development, it is essential (by dynamic necessity) that the religious voltage or temperature rise higher and higher in mankind as it proceeds towards totalization.

Second condition. Of all the forms of faith tried out as possibilities in the course of time, by the rising forces of religion, that form, and that alone (again by dynamic necessity), is destined to survive which will prove capable of stimulating (or 'activating') to their maximum the forces of self-evolution.

Precisely in so far as they derive from energetics, let me emphasize, these two propositions are independent of all philosophical or historical consideration. They have an absolute value for all the universe and for all time.

Let us try to see what they produce (that is, what happens) if we apply them to the particular case of Christian faith.

II. THE OUTSTANDING EVOLUTIVE VALUE OF CHRISTIANITY – EXCEPT IN RELATION TO THE IDEA OF CREATION

From the strictly dynamic (one might call it 'cosmo-motive') point of view adopted here, it is remarkable how far ahead of every form of belief is Christian faith, *properly understood*: and this for the excellent reason that, alone among all the other types of religion now confronting one another, it is proving capable of surviving (or even super-living) without distortion in a universe which, as conceived by our minds, has suddenly moved from the state of cosmos to that of cosmogenesis – and

---

from the religious point of view, the end of mankind could be brought closer by an increase in the magnetic force of Christ, the spiritual sun. Hence his invocation of the parousia in *Le Milieu Divin* (Collins, London, 1960, pp. 147-50; *The Divine Milieu*, Harper, New York, 1960, pp. 133-5).

it is proving capable, what is more, of so warming and illu-minating that cosmogenesis as literally to give it a face and a soul. The modern Christian, who has become simultaneously conscious *both* of the world's gradual centration on itself, *and* of the unique position occupied by the risen Christ at the pole of this convergent movement, now sees the entire process of evolution as ultimately and strictly *loving and lovable*. In conse-quence, when it comes to collaborating in the further advances of hominization, such a Christian, and such a one alone, proves ultimately to be animated by the most 'activating' of spiritual attractions that there can possibly be: and by that I mean the forces of *dilectio*, of love based on regard.

In as much as Christianity 'personalizes' cosmogenesis, it is, beyond doubt, irreplaceable and impregnable in the field of evolutive activance.

It may be objected that while the Christian faith (through its mysteries of Incarnation and even of Redemption) lends such charms to this world, at the same time it correspondingly robs it of all interest (and comes close to making it worthless for us) through its emphasis on God's complete self-sufficiency and, in consequence, on the complete contingence of creation.

And it is just at this point, in fact, that without our being sufficiently prepared for it, the apparently completely theo-retical and innocent problem of *participated being* suddenly enters a vitally concrete sphere – that of man's zest for action.

It is sound Scholastic philosophy, as everyone knows, that being, in the form of *Ens a se*,[2] is posited exhaustively and repletively, and instantaneously, at the ontological origin of all things. Following this in a second phase, all the rest (i.e. 'the world') appears in turn only as an entirely gratuitous supplement or addition: the guests at the divine banquet.

Strictly deduced from a particular metaphysics of potency and act, this thesis of creation's complete gratuitousness was

2. 'Being in itself.'

acceptable in the Thomistic framework of a static universe in which all the creature had to do was to accept his existence and effect his own salvation. By contrast, it becomes dangerous and virulent (because disheartening) as soon as, in a system of cosmogenesis, the 'participated being' we all are begins to wonder whether the radically contingent condition to which the theologians reduce it really justifies the pain and labour required for evolution. For, unless only individual happiness is to be sought at the term of existence (a form of happiness we have definitively rejected), how could man *fail to be robbed of his zest for action* by this alleged revelation of his radical uselessness ?[3]

In an earlier note,[4] some time ago, I emphasized the absolute necessity for Christianity, if it wishes to make an impact on our generation, to bring out the constructive, 'evolutive' aspect of the mystery of the Cross, and not simply its aspect as expiation or atonement.[5] I would like now – on equally good grounds, and in connexion with a point of dogma less noted

3. Père Teilhard would have been pleased to find his intuition confirmed by one of Cardinal de Bérulle's most important passages (which he never saw): 'The Father who is the original source of Godhead ... produces two divine persons in himself. And the Son ... completes his fertility in the production of a single divine person. And this third person, producing nothing eternal and uncreated, produces the Incarnate Word. And this Incarnate Word produces the order of grace and glory which ends in ... making us gods by participation' (*Les Grandeurs de Jésus*, Ed. Siffre, Paris, 1895, p. 272). The pleroma, that is God-man and a creation, not only assimilated by him, but participating in his divinity and the life of the Trinity, through the mankind which is its crown: such is the fertility of the Holy Spirit and the essential purpose of the universe, constituting its sovereign dignity.

4. 'Le Sens de la Croix' ('The Meaning of the Cross'), September 1952 (Note by Père Teilhard.)

5. This is the traditional point of view: the Redemption does not only atone for the offence: it produces a superabundance of grace; it manifests and creates a superaddition of love.

but even more fundamental – to record this considered opinion:

'At a time when man is awakening, apparently for ever, to consciousness of his planetary responsibilities and future, Christianity (for all the beauty of its gospel) would lose all religious value for us, if we had reason to suspect that by exalting the Creator it was robbing the universe of any spice of interest. For, on that ground alone, Christianity would cease to figure among the dynamically possible forms of belief.'

It would be no use to the Church, we must finally understand, to make the world lovable to our hearts if, from another angle, we saw that she was making it less desirable, or even contemptible, as a field for our effort.

If that is so, surely we should honestly try to rethink, in the new dimensions which the real has just assumed for us, the dogma of the Creator's complete *freedom* in the act of creation?

III. A CORRECTIVE TO CONTINGENCE: THE NOTION OF THE PLEROMA

If I have allowed myself so sharply to criticize the Scholastic notion of 'participation', it is not only (the reader will have understood) because it humiliates the man in me, but also, and equally, because it offends the Christian in me.

Let us, in fact, forget about '*Ens a se*' and '*Ens ab alio*'[6] and go back to the most authentic and most concrete expressions of Christian revelation and mysticism. At the heart of what we can learn or drink in from those, what do we find but the affirmation and the expression of a strictly bilateral and complementary relationship between the world and God? 'God creates by love', the Scholastics say, quite rightly. But what is this love, at once inexplicable in its subject and degrading for its object, which *is based on no need* (except the pleasure of

6. 'Being existing by itself' and 'Being existing by another.'

giving for the sake of giving)? If we reread St John and St Paul, we shall find that for them the existence of the world is accepted from the outset (too summarily, perhaps, for our taste) as an inevitable fact, or in any case as an accomplished fact. In both of them, on the other hand, what a sense we find of the absolute value of a cosmic drama in which God would indeed appear to have been ontologically involved even before his incarnation. And, in consequence, what emphasis on the pleroma and pleromization!

In truth, it is not the sense of contingence of the created but the sense of the mutual completion of the world and God which gives life to Christianity. And, that being so, if it is just this soul of 'complementarity' which Aristotelian ontology fails to get hold of, then we must do what the physicists do when mathematics is found wanting – change our geometry.

For example, we see that from a dynamic point of view[7] what comes first in the world for our thought, is not 'being' but 'the union which produces this being'. Let us, therefore, try to replace a metaphysics of *Esse* by a metaphysics of *Unire* (or of *Uniri*).[8] Treated in this genetic form, the problem of the co-existence and the complementarity of the created and the uncreated is undoubtedly solved in part: in so far, that is, as the two terms that are brought together, each in its own way, have an equal need both to exist in themselves and to be combined with each other,[9] so that the absolute maximum of possible union may be effected *in natura rerum*.

If this second way of thinking has not yet succeeded in

7. And by analogy with what happens in physics, where, as we now know, acceleration creates mass: which means that the moving object is posterior to motion. (Note by Père Teilhard.)

8. 'To be, to unite, to be united.'

9. Thus participated being would be defined not so much by its opposition to non-being as by its positive relation to God, its power of entering into communion. (Note by Père Teilhard.)

justifying to the believer the legitimate need, by which he lives, of contributing, through his eagerness to live, something irreplaceable to God, then we must not lose heart, but must search even more diligently.

Yet we must try not to deviate from our course; for, as I pointed out at the beginning, in such an affair the inflexible and omnivalent laws of energetics are categorical.

Sooner or later souls will end by giving themselves to the religion which activates them most as human beings.

In other words, the Christian faith can hope to dominate the earth tomorrow only if, while being already alone in a position to *amorize* the universe, it also proves itself to our reason to be alone capable of completely *valorizing* the stuff of the world and its evolution.

Unpublished, New York, 1 May 1953.

A SEQUEL TO THE PROBLEM OF HUMAN ORIGINS: THE PLURALITY OF INHABITED WORLDS

AFTER much debate, the question of human origins, in the terrestrial (i.e. restricted) form in which it was expressed in the nineteenth century, may be regarded as settled. A certain amount of skirmishing still goes on about a strict monogenism,[1] to which some theologians continue to cling (because it is required for their representation of original sin); but monogenism is becoming of less and less importance to scientists, because it is impatient of any experimental verification, and is, in fact, contrary to all the evidence provided by phyletics and genetics. In consequence there is no longer any doubt in competent circles but that man appeared on our planet, at the end of the Tertiary, in conformity with the general laws of speciation.

When expressed in strictly historical and terrestrial terms, we can safely say, the problem of man may well seem to have been solved. In reality, however, I believe it has been removed from that context to a higher degree of generalness (one might even say of 'universality') where it asserts itself again with fresh urgency and acuteness.

This is what seems quite apparent to me; and I would like to make it apparent 'in the proper quarters' by showing what results from the combination of three scientific propositions.

1. I say 'mono*genism*' advisedly (meaning a single original *couple*), and not mono*phyletism* (a single phylum, with an original cross-section indeterminate in area). (Note by Père Teilhard.)

Each one of these is solidly established on its own, but I do not think that we realize the explosive force of all three as soon as it occurs to us to link them together in sequence.

Proposition 1. Left to itself, under the influence of chance, matter tends to group itself into as large molecules as possible. And, experientially, life stands as the natural and normal continuation of this 'moleculization' process.

Proposition 2. In the same conditions, and once it has emerged from the inorganic, life continues naturally, and in a combined twofold movement, to become both complexified externally and more conscious internally; and this extends up to the psychological emergence of reflection. In other words, the now well-established fact of the appearance of man on earth in the Pliocene is simply the normal and *local* manifestation (in specially favourable conditions) of a property common to all 'terminally evolved' matter.

Proposition 3. There are millions of galaxies in the universe, in each of which matter has the same general composition and is going through essentially the same evolution as that inside our own Milky Way.

In competent circles, I repeat, there is now essential agreement on each of these three propositions taken individually. It just happens, however, that each one belongs to a discipline so far removed from that which includes the other two[2] that no one is professionally aware of the need to connect them: in this instance, our minds are still not accepting that 'two and two and two make six'.

And yet:

If it is true that the proteins (similar in this respect to every other chemical element) appear in the universe as soon as it is possible for them to do so, and wherever it is possible,

And *if,* when life has once taken hold on a star, it not only

2. Biochemistry, anthropology, and astronomy, respectively. (Note by Père Teilhard.)

propagates itself on that star but carries itself as far and to as high a degree as possible (that is, up to 'hominization' if it can),

And *if*, in addition, there are thousands of millions of solar systems in the world in which life has equal chances of being born and becoming hominized,

Then, our minds cannot resist the inevitable conclusion that were we, by chance, to possess plates that were sensitive to the specific radiation of the 'noospheres' scattered thoughout space, it would be *practically certain* that what we saw registered on them would be a cloud of thinking stars.

In Fontenelle's day it was possible to amuse oneself with the still purely arbitrary idea of the plurality of inhabited worlds.[3]

The position is now completely and permanently reversed. There has been such a simultaneous advance in our physical and biological knowledge that what was pure imagination in the time of Louis XIV is seen by us in the twentieth century to be *by a long way the most probable* alternative.

In other words, considering what we now know about the number of 'worlds' and their internal evolution, the idea of *a single* hominized[4] *planet* in the universe has already become in fact (without our generally realizing it) almost as *inconceivable* as that of a man who appeared with no genetic relationship to the rest of the earth's animal population.

3. Just as, in the time of Copernicus, one could with the hypothesis (still regarded as a quaint conceit) that it was not the sun but the earth that revolved in the firmament. (Note by Père Teilhard.)

4. 'Mankind' ('humanity', 'human race') and 'hominized', it must be clear, are used here as synonymous with 'psychically *reflected* life'. We have, it is true, no idea either of the chemistry or the morphology peculiar to the various extra-terrestrial forms of life. However, there is every reason to believe that should material contact be effected between two 'hominized' planets, they would be able, at least through their noospheres, to understand one another, combine and be synthesized with one another. (Note by Père Teilhard.)

At an average of (at least) one human race per galaxy, that makes a total of millions of human races dotted all over the heavens.

Confronted with this fantastic multiplicity of astral centres of 'immortal life', how is theology going to react, if it is to satisfy the anxious expectations and hopes of all who wish to continue to worship God 'in spirit and in truth'? It obviously cannot go on much longer offering as the only *dogmatically certain* thesis one (that of the uniqueness in the universe of terrestrial mankind) which our experience rejects as *improbable*.

What then? At this dangerous choice of roads, we must try to determine not only what must be absolutely avoided by 'apologists' but also what positive action we believers must henceforth take if we are not to be overcome by the situation.

I. WHAT APOLOGETICS MUST AVOID

When a theologian is confronted with the growing scientific probability of multiple 'centres of thought' distributed throughout the world, he can immediately see two easy (though deceptive) ways of avoiding the problem, and they are all the more attractive in that he has already followed them in the past.

He can decide either that, alone among all the inhabited planets, earth has known original sin and has needed to be redeemed; or, accepting the hypothesis of a universal original sin, he can assume that the Incarnation was effected only on earth, the other mankinds being, in addition, duly 'informed' of it in some way (!?).

Or, finally, he can rely on the odds (very high odds, too) against any contact ever being made, by way of direct experiment,[5] between earth and other thinking stars, and so maintain,

5. Because of excessive distance in space, or non-coincidence in time. (Note by Père Teilhard.)

against all probability,[6] that earth alone in the universe is inhabited. And this simply means digging in his heels and saying that 'the problem does not exist'.

It calls for no great learning to see and feel that in the present state of our knowledge about the dimensions of the universe and the nature of life:

a. The first of these three solutions is scientifically 'absurd' – in as much as it implies that death (the theological index of the presence of original sin) might not exist at certain points in the universe – in spite of our certain knowledge that those points are subject to the same physico-chemical laws as earth.[7]

b. The second is 'ridiculous', particularly when one considers the enormous number of stars to be 'informed' (miraculously?) and their distance from one another in space and time.

c. And finally the third is 'humiliating' – in as much as it would be one more instance of the Church apparently taking refuge in the unverifiable to protect the dogma.

The sudden enlargement, as an experiential fact, of the 'spiritual' dimensions of the universe means that we now have a difficulty to face in our faith; and if we are to have a dignified and rewarding way of neutralizing the difficulty, we absolutely must find something better than such loopholes. Where shall we find it?

II. POSITIVE ACTION

No matter how great a probability may be, we must be careful not to treat it as a certainty – that is obvious. The plurality of

6. Precisely as in the case of monogenism. (Note by Père Teilhard.)

7. It is embarrassing (unless it was meant as a joke) to read in *Time* (15 September 1952) the advice given by a teacher of theology (Fr. Francis J. Connell, Dean of Theology) to be wary of pilots of 'flying saucers': if they landed from a planet not affected by original sin, they would be *unkillable*. (Note by Père Teilhard.)

extra-terrestrial 'mankinds' has not yet been (and, very likely, never will be) established by direct communication. There is no question, then, of having to begin work on a theology for these unknown worlds. We must at least, however, endeavour to make our classical theology open to (I was on the point of saying 'blossom into') the possibility (a positive possibility) of their existence and their presence.

That, if I am not mistaken, is something that can certainly be done – provided only that, following two currents of thought, both characteristic of our time, we make ourselves familiar, intellectually and mystically, with these two notions:

both of *universe* psychically convergent on itself, through the whole of itself (as a result of the evolutive process known as 'complexification-consciousness');[8]

and of *Christ universalized* in his operation, in virtue of, and by virtue of, his resurrection.

For ultimately, if, on the one hand, all reflected substance produced in the course of time by the universe does truly tend, in the eyes of the scientist, to concentrate upon itself; and if, on the other hand, in the eyes of the believer, Christ, also by nature, is he who centres, and in whom is centred, the entire universe – then we can indeed be easy in our minds.

For, *even* if there are actually (as is now *more probable*) millions of 'inhabited worlds' in the firmament, the fundamental situation is still unchanged for the Christian (or, rather, it becomes enormously more important) in as much as he can regard these millions as reinforcing and glorifying the same unity as before.

No doubt (as happened earlier at the end of geocentrism) it is inevitable that the end of 'monogeism'[9] may well oblige us

8. On which see, for example, 'The Reflection of Energy'. (Note by Père Teilhard.) (In *Activation of Energy*, Collins, London, 1970, and Harcourt Brace Jovanovich, New York, 1971.)

9. Or perhaps one should say 'geo-monism'? (Note by Père Teilhard.)

to revise a good many of our theological 'representations' and make them more flexible; but these adjustments matter little provided that, ever more structurally and dynamically coherent with all we are now discovering in connexion with cosmogenesis, one thing remains solidly established: the dogma which sums up all dogmas:

'*In Eo Omnia constant.*'[10]

LATER NOTE (BY THE AUTHOR)

J.M. hypothesis.[11] 'A Christified human noosphere which gradually extends over the world.' Attractive, but contrary to the facts: millions of galaxies, now existing
  already extinct

10. 'In him all things hold together' (Col. 1:17).

11. J. M. hypothesis, as reformulated and completed since 1953: In the whole universe, as on earth, there is a *before* the Incarnation and an *after*. For Christ's work of divinization to spread over the universe, it is sufficient to assume that God has raised up on each thinking planet (and continues to do so until the end) prophets and priests to whom knowledge of the redemptive Incarnation has been revealed and its grace communicated. Just like Melchizedek, a priest risen from the directly chosen tribe, they have participated, or will participate, within the unfolding of space-time, in the priesthood of the Incarnate Word; receiving the power to celebrate his sacrifice, to consecrate the Host and to administer the eucharist and the sacraments, either in prefiguration (as, on earth, before the Incarnation), or as a continuation of the Last Supper.

For the universe is so perfectly one that the Son of God has only to enter into it once to occupy and permeate it in its entirety with his filiating grace.

By taking a human nature, the Word was 'cosmified'. He had to be born but once of the Virgin Mary to make his own and divinize the whole of creation.

Just as Christ's birth is cosmic, so are his passion and death. 'Christ being raised from the dead will never die again' (Romans 6:9) because the mysteries of Christ embrace, in their extension and their perfection, the whole development of the world which is strictly *one*.

at unattainable distances: even electro-magnetically their distance outruns the life of mankind!

The only solution: in the two combined ideas:

a. of convergent universe (=centred)

b. of Christ (3rd nature)[12] centre of the universe.

Unpublished, New York, 5 June 1953.

12. A cosmic nature, enabling him to centre all the lives which constitute a pleroma extended to the galaxies.

THE GOD
OF EVOLUTION

Dᴜʀɪɴɢ these last years I have tried, in a series of short memoranda[1] to pin down and define the exact reason why Christianity, in spite of a certain renewal of its grip on back-ward-looking (or undeveloped[2]) circles in the world, is de-cidedly and obviously losing its reputation with the most influential and most progressive portion of mankind and ceas-ing to appeal to it. Not only among the Gentiles or the rank and file of the faithful, but even in the religious orders them-selves, Christianity still to some degree provides a *shelter* for the 'modern soul', but it no longer *clothes* it, nor *satisfies* it, nor *leads* it. Something has gone wrong – and so something, in the area of faith and religion, must be supplied without delay on this planet. The question is, what is it we are looking for?

It is a question that is asked on all sides, and I shall try once again to answer it by establishing, in a short sequence of linked propositions, the reality of a phenomenon whose manifest existence has been haunting me for what will soon be half a century. I mean the rise (irresistible and yet still unrecognized) over our horizon of what one might call a God (*the* God) of evolution.

I. THE 'EVOLUTION' EVENT

I am becoming more and more convinced that at the funda-mental root of the multiple currents and conflicts that are now

1. 'The Heart of the Problem' (1950) in *The Future of Man* (Collins, London, and Harper & Row, New York, 1964); 'The Meaning of the Cross' (1952), and 'The Contingence of the Universe' (1953), above, pp. 212 and 221.

2. Père Teilhard uses the English word.

convulsing the human mass we must place our generation's gradual awakening to consciousness of a movement which is cosmic in breadth and organicity: a movement which, whether we welcome it or not, is drawing us, through the relentless building up in our minds of a common *Weltanschauung*, towards some 'ultra-human' lying ahead in time.

A century ago evolution (so-called) could still be regarded as a mere local hypothesis, framed to meet the problem of the origin of species (and, more particularly, that of human origins). Since that time, however, we cannot avoid recognizing that it has included and now dominates the whole of our experience. 'Darwinism' and 'transformism' are words that already have only an historical interest. From the lowest and least stable nuclear elements up to the highest living beings, we now realize, nothing exists, nothing in nature can be an object of scientific thought except as a function of a vast and single combined process of 'corpusculization' and 'complexification', in the course of which can be distinguished the phases of a gradual and irreversible 'interiorization' (development of consciousness) of what we call (without knowing what it is) matter.

a. First, at the very bottom, and in vast numbers, we have relatively simple particles (corpuscles), which are still (at least apparently) *unconscious*: Pre-life.

b. Next, following on the emergence of life, and in relatively small numbers, we have beings that are *simply conscious*.

c. And now (right now!) we have beings that have suddenly become *conscious of becoming every day a little more conscious* as a result of 'co-reflection'.

This is the position we have reached.

As I said before, evolution has in a few years invaded the whole field of our experience; but, what is more, since we can feel ourselves swept up and sucked up in its convergent flood, this evolution is giving new value, as material for our action, to the whole domain of existence: precisely in as much as the appearance of a peak of unification at the higher term of cosmic ferment is now objectively providing human aspirations (for the first time in the course of history) with an absolute direction and an absolute end.

From this arises, *ipso facto*, the general maladjustment we see on all sides in the old moulds in which either morality or religion is contained.

II. THE DIVINE IN EVOLUTION

We still hear it said that the fact that we now see the universe not as a cosmos but henceforth as a cosmogenesis in no way affects the idea we used to be able to form of the Author of all things. 'As though it made any difference to God', is a common objection, 'whether he creates *instantaneously* or *evolutively*'.

I shall not try to discuss now the notion (or pseudo-notion) of 'instantaneous creation', nor dwell on the reasons which make me suspect the presence of an ontological contradiction latent in this association of the two words.

On the other hand I must emphasize with all the power at my command the following cardinal point:

While, in the case of a static world, the creator (the efficient cause) is still, on any theory, *structurally* independent of his work, and in consequence, without any definable basis to his immanence – in the case of a world which is by nature evolutive, the contrary is true: God is not conceivable (either structurally or dynamically) except in so far as he coincides with (as a sort of 'formal' cause), but without being lost in, the centre of convergence of cosmogenesis. I say, advisedly, either structurally or dynamically: because, if God did not appear to us now at this supreme and exact point at which we see that nature is finally held together, our capacity to love would inevitably gravitate not towards him but (a situation we could not possibly accept) towards some other 'God'.

Ever since Aristotle there have been almost continual attempts to construct 'models' of God on the lines of an outside Prime Mover, acting *a retro*.[3] Since the emergence in our consciousness of the 'sense of evolution' it has become physically impossible for us to conceive or worship anything but an organic Prime-Mover God, *ab ante*.[4]

In future only a God who is functionally and totally 'Omega' can satisfy us.

Where, then, shall we find such a God? And who will at last give evolution *its own* God?

III. THE CHRISTIC ADVENT AND EVENT

As a result, then, of life's very recent passing through a new critical point in the course of its development,[5] no older religious form or formulation can any longer (either factually or logically) satisfy to the full our need and capacity for worship – satisfy, I mean, what has now become permanently their specifically human quality. So true is this, that a 'religion of the future' (definable as a 'religion of evolution') cannot fail to appear before long: a new mysticism, the germ of which (as happens when anything is born) must be recognizable somewhere in our environment, *here and now*.

The more one considers this psycho-biological situation, the more clearly one can distinguish the *universal* meaning and importance of what may legitimately be called the 'Christic advent'.

3. 'Starting from the beginning.'
4. 'Drawing us ahead.'
5. This critical point being man's awakening to consciousness of a movement in which human consciousness converges upon itself. (Note by Père Teilhard.)

The gospel tells us that Christ once asked his disciples: '*Quem dicunt esse Filium hominis?*'[6] To which Peter impetuously answered: '*Tu es Christus, Filius Dei vivi*'[7] – which was both an answer and no answer, since it still left the question of knowing what exactly is 'the true living God'.

Consider then: from the earliest days of the Church, has not the whole history of Christian thought been one long, slow and persistent exploration of Peter's testimony to the Man-Jesus?

An extraordinary and absolutely unique phenomenon: as the centuries go by, all the great figures of prophets invariably become blurred or are 'mythologized' in human consciousness – Christ, on the other hand, and Christ alone, as time passes, becomes a more and more real being for a particularly vigorous section of mankind; and this as a result of a twofold process which, paradoxically, continually both personalizes and universalizes him more fully as the years go by. For millions and millions of believers (representing the most consciously aware of human beings), Christ has never ceased since his first coming to re-emerge from every crisis of history with more immediacy, more urgency and greater penetrative power than ever before.

If, then, he is to be able to offer himself once again to our new world as the 'new God' for whom we are looking, what does he still lack?

Two things, to my mind, and two only.

The first is this: that in a universe in which we can no longer seriously entertain the idea that thought is an exclusively terrestrial phenomenon, Christ must no longer be *constitutionally* restricted in his operation to a mere 'redemption' of our planet.

6. 'Whom do they say is the Son of man?'

7. 'You are the Christ, the Son of the living God.' The exact wording of the Vulgate (Matt. 16:15-16) is: '*Dicit illis Jesus: Vos autem quem me esse dicitis? Respondens Simon Petrus dixit: Tu es Christus Filius Dei vivi.*'

And the second: that in a universe in which we can now see that everything is co-reflective along a single axis, Christ must no longer be offered to our worship (in consequence of a subtle and pernicious confusion between 'super-natural' and 'extra-natural') as a peak distinct from, and a rival to, that to which the biologically continued slope of anthropogenesis is leading us.

In the eyes of everyone who is alive to the reality of the cosmic movement of complexity-consciousness which produces us, Christ, as still presented to the world by classical theology, is both too confined (localized) astronomically, and evolutively too extrinsic, to be able to 'cephalize' the universe as we now see it.

And further, there is undoubtedly a most revealing correspondence between the shapes (the pattern[8]) of the two confronting Omegas: that postulated by modern science, and that experienced by Christian mysticism. A correspondence – and one might even say a parity! For Christ would not still be the Consummator so passionately described by St Paul if he did not take on precisely the attributes of the astonishing cosmic pole already potentially (if not as yet explicitly) demanded by our new knowledge of the world: the pole at whose peak the progress of evolution must finally converge.

Prediction and extrapolation, it is true, are always dangerous.

Nevertheless, it is surely impossible in the present circumstances not to believe that Christ's gradual rise in human consciousness cannot continue much longer without there being produced, in our spiritual climate, the revolutionary event of his coincidence with the definitely foreseeable centre of a terrestrial co-reflection (and, more generally, of the assumed focus of all reflection in the universe).

Forced together ever more closely by the progress of homin-ization, and drawn together even more by a fundamental

8. Père Teilhard uses the English word.

identity, the two Omegas (let me emphasize again), the Omegas of experience and of faith, are undoubtedly on the point of reacting upon one another in human consciousness, and finally of *being synthesized*: the cosmic being about fantastically to magnify the Christic; and the Christic (astonishing though it may seem) to amorize (which means to energize to the maximum[9]) the entire cosmic.

It is, in truth, an inevitable 'implosive' meeting; and its probable effect will soon be to weld together science and mysticism in a great tide of released evolutive power – centred around a Christ at last, two thousand years after Peter's confession, identified[10] by the work of centuries as the ultimate summit (that is, the only possible God) of an evolution definitively recognized as a movement of convergence.

That is what I foresee.

And that is what I am waiting for.

At the Equator, 25 October (Christ the King) 1953. Published in *Cahier VI* of the *Fondation Teilhard de Chardin* (Ed. du Seuil, Paris, 1968).

9. And, in a way, to 'raise it to incandescence'. (Note by Père Teilhard.)

10. By direct extension of his theandric attributes, and without thereby annihilating his historical reality. (Note by Père Teilhard.)

MY LITANY

A manuscript litany found, at Père Teilhard's death, written on both sides of a picture of the radiant heart of Christ. The picture stood on his desk. The litany appears to belong to the same period as 'The God of Evolution'.

On the front: The God of evolution
The Christic, the Trans-Christ

Jesus { Heart of the world / Essence / Motor } { of evolution

On the back: Sacred Heart
Introibo ad altare Dei[1]
(penetrate the presence)

Sacred Heart	The motor of evolution
	The heart of evolution
Trans (Christ)	The heart of matter
The 'altar' of God	The centre of Jesus
The heart of the world's heart	The golden glow[2]
The heart of God (core[3])	The world-zest
The activant of Christianity	The essence of all energy
	The cosmic curve
	The heart of God
	The issue of cosmogenesis
The focus, pole	The tide of cosmic convergence
	The God of evolution
	The U.[4] Jesus

1. 'I will go up to the altar of God.' At that time, the priest's opening words at the foot of the altar-steps.
2. In English. 3. In English.
4. Probably, the universal Jesus.

The psychic motor

The focus of all reflection
Axis {of the cosmic vortex
and issue (acme)
Heart of the world's heart

Focus of ultimate and
universal energy
Centre of the cosmic
sphere of cosmogenesis
Heart of Jesus, heart of
evolution, unite me to
yourself (etc.)

INDEX

Above, the; meeting with the Ahead, 206, 206n; synthesis with the Ahead in the Cross, 219; transcendent God of, 212

act; and potency, 29, 32, 224; true, 110-11

action; and immortality, 110; problem of, 110-11

Adam, 36, 37, 38, 50, 81; and contemporary science, 46, 47, 79; denial of historicity, 39n; and Eve, 48, 49, 50, 51, 52, 79, 86; first, 39, 41, 50, 51; instantaneous creation of and the Fall: incomprehensibility of theory, 191-2, 194; rejection of individual, 52, 210; relationship to Christ, 190n; second, 41, 43, 192; of theologians, 210; universalizing of, 39

agape, 24n

Ahead, the; and the Above, 206, 206n; evolutive God of, 212

Alexandrian school, 45; creation and redemption in universe of, 197; Logos of, 59, 180; on original sin, 191n, 194

amorization, 186, 201; by Christianity, 228; of cosmic Omega by Christic Omega, 243; of evolution, 208; of universe, 218

Annapurna, Mt., 222

Annunciation, 66

anthropocentrism, 106n; and Christianity, 137; and theocentrism, 185

anthropogenesis, 141, 208, 211; Christianity and, 161, 175; man's involvement in, 174; Omega at peak of, 143, 242; planetary, 200

anthropology, 140

anthropomorphism; and Christianity, 136, 137; primitive, 200

apologetics and the miracle, 119-20, 167

Aristotle, 227, 240

Ascension, 162

ascesis, Christian, 169-70

atom, primitive, 204

atomicity; original sin effect of, 197n; of stuff of the cosmos, 187, 187n

Augustine, St, 145

Australian aborigines, 46

baptism, 18, 81; full mystery of, 85; necessity, 149n; new concept, 146; and original sin as a state, 196-7

Barthianism, 215

Baumgartner, Père Charles, 39n

beatitude, 16, 177

becoming, general laws of, 32-3

being; appearance of, 33, 52; and creative transformation, 23; 'in itself', 224; metaphysics of, 178, 227; personalized, 114; Scholasticism and, 21, 21n; unification in Christ, 52

belief, see faith

Bérulle, Pierre de, 198n, 225n, 228n

Bible, 38, 39, 48, 81

biogenesis, 204

biology, 100, 141; and miracles, 29

biosphere, 100, 204

Blondel, Maurice, 110

Bonsirven, J., 139

boredom, 206

brain, 24

Buddhism, 121; neo-, 122n

Catholicism; and Christianity, 168; and the world and matter, 128. See Christianity, Church

cephalization; Church and law of, 153, 168; of universe by Christ, 242

chance, 105, 218

charity, 72-3; love of evolution and reinterpretation of, 184-5; primacy, 152

chastity, 92

Christ; actualizing of, 32; and Adam, 41-2, 43, 190, 190n; coincidence with Omega, 143-4, 148, 180, 181, 242-3; consummated, 69, 70; consummator,